3605335660

D1101405

7556

MORAL THEOLOGY IN THE MODERN WORLD

MORAL THEOLOGY
IN THE
MODERN WORLD

By

LINDSAY DEWAR

Rector of Much Hadham, Herts.
Honorary Canon of St. Albans
Fellow of King's College, London

LONDON
A. R. MOWBRAY & Co. LIMITED

© *A. R. Mowbray & Co. Limited, 1964*

First published in 1964

ST. AUGUSTINE'S COLLEGE
LIBRARY
CANTERBURY

PRINTED IN GREAT BRITAIN BY
A. R. MOWBRAY & CO. LIMITED IN THE CITY OF OXFORD
3678

INTRODUCTION

THE prevailing confusion of moral standards will hardly be denied by anybody. Nor are the reasons for it obscure. It is partly due (at least so far as the western world is concerned) to the weakening of belief in the basic doctrines of the Christian creed, notably belief in the Incarnation, which carries with it belief in the irrefragable authority of our Lord's moral teaching. It is also partly due to the rise of the scientific age, when the tendency has been to appeal first and foremost not to authority but to experimentation. Thus, for many minds to-day, questions of morality, like everything else, must be settled not by authority, however venerable, but by experiment.

These influences have made themselves felt even on professedly Christian moralists, some of whom are inclined to jettison the whole traditional moral teaching of the Church, and to start anew on empirical lines to found a new Christian morality, which shall be more in keeping with the temper of the times.

I have set out to write this book in order to examine, as carefully and impartially as I could, this modern empirical approach to questions of Christian ethics and moral theology. I have tried to do justice to the claim—which I believe to be a fair claim—that, in the past, moral theology has given insufficient attention to empirical data. This being an empirical and scientific age, we must see that our moral thinking is up-to-date. But as I have proceeded in my writing I have found myself forced back again and again to the conception of moral law—which is the bugbear of some of our modern Christian moralists. And this has driven me to the recognition of the fact that it is absolutely essential to distinguish between law on the one hand and legalism on the other. That the latter is harmful and less than Christian I have no wish to deny; but it is, in my view, quite disastrous to fail to distinguish between the two, as many modern writers do. One of the primary purposes of this book is to attempt to show how and where this line of distinction should be drawn. Until this all-important task has been achieved, it is useless to expect a revival of moral theology —the Cinderella of modern theological studies—in the modern world; and we shall continue to be subject to the present moral confusion of voices claiming to be Christian. It is often stated that the rising generation will have nothing to do with moral laws and standards, and that the Church will never win it until she abandons them. But there is clear evidence that what the rising generation seeks is, in fact, a stable moral authority on which to rest. Every psychiatrist knows that. Those modern moralists, therefore, who in the name of our Lord are quick to condemn the traditional basis of Christian morals for nearly two thousand years may not unfairly be accused of making it harder and not easier for the young whom they seek to help.

I have not, however, been concerned to draw a similar line of demarcation between moral theology and Christian ethics; and if any critic should complain that much of the contents of this book concern the latter rather than the former, I shall be quite unmoved. On any showing they both cover a good deal of the same ground. The distinction between them is mainly one of convention. Moral theology is rather more practical in its approach to ethical questions, being concerned to give specific guidance in the living of the Christian life. Hence, as I think, it should certainly include what has been called Ascetical Theology, the study of the growth and development of the soul pressing on unto perfection. As we shall see, this has always been part of the Anglican tradition in moral theology. It is the best safeguard against that kind of debased moral theology which has been described as a set of 'rules for the breaking of rules,'[1] and which is too much concerned with minimum standards. It is, however, a serious mistake to suppose that moral theology is necessarily like this. We not only need moral principles to guide us through life, but we also need to know how to apply them in the practical business of living. That is the sum and substance of moral theology. Consequently every seriously-minded person is involved in moral theology, whether he is aware of it or not.

I wish to thank the Reverend R. H. Preston, Canon-Residentiary of Manchester Cathedral, for reading the first draft of this book, and for the helpful criticisms which he passed upon it, to which I have given good heed. Although I have been obliged to disagree with him on some important questions, I recognize that I am greatly indebted to him for his stimulating comments without which this book would certainly have been even less adequate than it is. I also wish to thank Dr. E. A. Bennet, M.D., D.P.M., for reading in proof Chapters 5 and 7 and giving me the benefit of his advice thereon. Needless to say, neither he nor Canon Preston is responsible for anything which I have written.

Although I have inevitably written this book from an Anglican point of view, I have not written it primarily *for* members of the Anglican communion. It deals with matters which are of vital concern to all Christians, both Catholic and Protestant, and I have tried to approach these problems in such a way as to be of assistance to all who believe in the Incarnation of our Lord Jesus Christ, whatever their particular tradition may be.

LINDSAY DEWAR.

MUCH HADHAM RECTORY,
HERTS.

---

[1] C. F. D'Arcy: *Christian Ethics and Modern Thought*, p. 103.

CONTENTS

MORAL THEOLOGY IN THE MODERN WORLD

CHAPTER 1

The Traditional Approach to Moral Theology

The traditional approach to moral theology is clearly bound up with the influence of Roman law upon Christian doctrine and morals. This influence was consolidated in the codification effected under Justinian in the *Institutes*, the *Digest* and the *Code*. It is not now to our purpose to enter into the difficult and still debated question as to how far the work of Justinian gives a correct historical picture of the development of Roman law—that is to say, how much that is later is read back into that which was earlier. It is sufficient for our purpose to accept the Justinian codification of law as it stands and to examine its bearing upon the development of Christian moral theology.

The Justinian code was both influenced by Christianity and in its turn influenced it. Thus, for example, the severity of the ancient Roman law as witnessed in the power of life and death allowed to a paterfamilias over his offspring was mollified by the Christian doctrine of the value of each individual soul as belonging to God and precious in his eyes. The influence of the Stoic doctrine of human equality was also doubtless powerful here. On the other hand, the influence of Justinian's code on moral theology was strong, especially in two respects. In the first place, it led to an approach to moral questions which was characteristic of the Old Testament rather than the New Testament in many respects. There grew up alongside the *Corpus Juris Civilis* a *Corpus Juris Canonici*, and there was thus imparted to moral theology a legal, not to say a legalist, bias. In view of the anti-legalist bias of the New Testament this is surprising, but the fact is undeniable.

1

In the second place, the concept of *ius naturale* whether identified with or related to *ius gentium* became a basic principle of moral theology. As we find it in Justinian, it is certainly vague, and it did not possess the significance later ascribed to it, which enabled it to over-ride the civil law. Nevertheless, it pointed to the belief that law is something more fundamental than convention; that, in terms of Greek thought, it is *phusis* and not *nomos*.

There was another influence upon the traditional Christian moral teaching and practice the effect of which is far harder to estimate, and that is the influence of Stoicism. It is a commonplace to say that, as creeds, Stoicism and Christianity are poles apart. However, as Bishop Lightfoot pointed out, Stoicism is 'the most incongruous, the most self-contradictory, of all philosophic systems. With a gross and material pantheism it unites the most vivid impressions of the fatherly love and providence of God.'[1] It thus became possible for terms and phrases to be employed by the Stoics about the dignity of man and human reason which were easily susceptible of a Christian interpretation; and doubtless in this sense they did affect the spread of Christian ethical ideas by preparing the way for them. At the same time, it is unnecessary to postulate more than this, if the basic ideas of the Natural Law which ultimately prevailed in Christendom can be found, as we believe they can be found, in the New Testament. It is certainly a gross exaggeration to say that the social teaching of Stoicism 'forms a complete analogy with the sociological thought of Christianity.'[2]

It was this conception of Natural Law which, in course of time, led to a basic revolution in the Christian approach to life and to the ultimate establishing of what became the traditional approach to moral theology. Let us follow the course of its development, beginning with the New Testament.

---

[1] *Commentary on Philippians*, p. 298.
[2] E. Troeltsch: *The Social Teaching of the Christian Church* (E.T.), p. 65.

In the New Testament we find, as we should expect, the main emphasis upon the new revelation in Christ, manifested in the making of a new covenant between God and 'the Israel of God' (*Gal.* 6. 16). This covenant, although it replaced the Old Covenant, did not destroy it, but completed it and brought it to fruition. Thus St. Paul, after a strong attack upon the old law of works embodied in the Old Covenant, repudiates strongly the suggestion that he is undermining the teaching of the Jewish Law (*Rom.* 3. 31). What is more, there is no doubt at all that St. Paul recognizes that entirely outside the confines of the Jewish Law there is a Gentile Law which was given them by God. He says: 'When Gentiles who do not possess the law carry out its precepts by the light of nature, then, although they have no law, they are their own law, for they display the effect of the law inscribed on their hearts' (*Rom.* 2. 14). There are other passages in his letters where the Apostle expresses the same view. Thus, in his discussion on the behaviour of women, he says: 'Does not even nature itself teach you, that, if a man have long hair, it is a dishonour to him? But if a woman have long hair, it is a glory to her; for her hair is given her for a covering' (1 *Cor.* 2. 14 & 15). Similarly, St. Peter assumes that even pagans have the capacity for sound moral judgement. He writes: 'Let all your behaviour be such as even pagans can recognize as good, and then, whereas they malign you as criminals now, they will come to see for themselves that you live good lives'[1] (1 *Peter* 2. 12). Teaching of this kind was not a novelty for a Jew of later times; for the rabbis certainly taught by the end of the second century that the fundamental laws were given to Noah, and even to Adam.[2] St. Paul may well have heard something like it from Gamaliel. But what is far more important he certainly received it from Christ; for it is presupposed in a great deal of our Lord's teaching, especially

---

[1] *New English Bible, ad loc.*   [2] See Strack-Billerbeck on Romans 2. 14.

in his teaching by parables. Most of these, as Quick[1] pointed out, are not allegories, but plain matter of fact stories about the way in which normal human beings behave all the world over. On the basis of such behaviour our Lord argues to the character of God who made these men and women—an *a fortiori* argument. Thus, for example, he says: 'If ye then, being evil, know how to give good gifts unto your children, how much more shall your Father which is in heaven give good things to them that ask him?' (*Matt.* 7. 11). The constant implication in these stories is that there is in the common man a power of moral judgement and behaviour which is 'natural.' Likewise, to take another example, in his teaching about marriage, our Lord takes his hearers back behind the Law of Moses to the Law of God 'in the beginning.'

Thus it is fair to say that in the New Testament we find the seeds of the full-blown doctrine of Natural Law as it finally developed. Unfortunately, however, what might have been a comparatively rapid growth was seriously retarded by the cold winds of state persecution which soon blew upon the young Church, and which led to strong antagonism between Christians and pagans, and made it difficult for the former to appreciate the virtues of their persecutors.

For many of the early Fathers natural institutions such as the state were imposed by God upon man as a punishment for his sin. Thus, for example, Irenaeus wrote: 'For since man by departing from God reached such a pitch of fury as even to look upon his brother as an enemy and engage without fear in every kind of restless conduct and murder and avarice, God imposed upon man the fear of man, as they did not acknowledge the fear of God, in order that, being subjected to the authority of men and kept under restraint by their laws, they might attain to some degree of

---

[1] O. C. Quick: *The Realism of Christ's Parables* (1925), *passim.*

justice by their laws and exercise mutual forbearance through dread of the sword.'[1] Even when Constantine took the Church under his protection and Church and State became assimilated, there was still a deep pessimism underlying the Christian attitude to the world. This is clearly seen in St. Augustine's great work, *The City of God*, which exerted such a powerful influence upon Christian thinking. Although the *civitas terrena* cannot be identified with any particular existent, it lies behind all that transpires in the world. In Bishop Creighton's famous expression, it is 'human society organizing itself apart from God.' Its influence on earth is all pervading, and this gives a pessimistic tone to much of Augustine's thought. This is intelligible enough since he was writing at a time when, by reason of the fall of Rome, the civilized world seemed to be tumbling into ruins.

In course of time, however, this mood passed, and we find a slow revolution of thought which led, in fact, to a return to New Testament teaching, and the development and springing to life of those seeds of Natural Law doctrine which had apparently lain dormant for centuries.

The true fashioner of the full doctrine of Natural Law, on which the traditional moral theology is based, was St. Thomas Aquinas. We must, therefore, carefully consider his teaching on this matter, and its relevance for moral theology. Law, according to Aquinas, is firmly based on reason. Law means the rule and measure of human actions, and this means that it is essentially rational, since it is the function of reason to direct towards an end.[2] He divides Law into four kinds: Eternal Law, Natural Law, Divine Law embodied in the Holy Scriptures, and Human Law. Eternal Law exists in the mind of the Ruler and Governor of the universe, who ordereth all things, and who, as St. Paul says, calls those things which are not as though they were.[3] Therefore, since all things are subject to the divine

[1] Irenaeus: *Adv. Haer.* V. 24.   [2] S.T. 1a–2ae. Q. 90. a. 1.   [3] *Ibid.* Q. 91. a. 1.

Providence, it is clear that all things participate in some degree in the eternal law, in so far as they derive from it certain inclinations to those actions and aims which are proper to them. Of all others, however, rational creatures are subject to divine Providence in a higher way; being themselves made participators in Providence itself, in that they control their own actions and the actions of others. Therefore they share in the divine reason itself through which they have a natural inclination to such actions and ends as are fitting. This participation in the eternal law by rational creatures is called the *natural law*. Thus when the Psalmist said: 'Sacrifice the sacrifice of justice,' as though to those who were asking what are works of justice, he adds: 'Many say, Who shows us what is good?' and replies to the questioner saying: 'the light of thy countenance, Lord, is signed upon us'; as though the light of natural reason by which we discern good from evil and which is the Natural Law were nothing else than the impression of the divine light in us. Thus it is clear that the natural law is nothing less than the participation of the rational creature in the eternal law.[1]

Aquinas teaches that the Natural Law is immutable in respect of the basic precepts of that law, but he points out that something may be predicated of the Natural Law in two different ways. On the one hand it may be said that nature inclines us to some course of action positively—e.g. that we should not injure another person gratuitously, which no normal person wishes to do. On the other hand it may be said that nature inclines us negatively to some course of action, and thereby may be said to approve it. This makes it possible for reason to lead us to make additions to the positive precepts of the Natural Law. For instance, to lead us to approve the wearing of clothes, or the holding

[1] S.T. 1a–2ae. Q. 91. a. 2.

of private possessions. Furthermore, St. Thomas argues that the Natural Law contains secondary precepts which we can deduce from the general principles just as in the case of speculative thought we draw conclusions from axioms and first principles. He thinks that, in the case of the Natural Law—which, of course, is solely concerned with practical matters—there are three main groups of secondary precepts. The first is that which man shares with everything, which is the condition which Spinoza called *Conatus in se perseverare* and which, in the case of man, is commonly called the instinct of self-preservation. The second is shared by man with the lower animals, viz. the tendency to reproduce his kind and to care for his offspring. The third is peculiar to man and is the desire to know God and to live in peaceful communion with him and with one's fellows. Unfortunately, these secondary precepts may be obscured or, in some cases, even obliterated by a depraved mind or by evil custom or bad habit.[1]

It may be objected—it is frequently objected to-day—that in the Thomist conception of Natural Law there is a great deal of vagueness, so that its usefulness in practice is far less than some of its supporters claim. Indeed, some would even go so far as to argue that for practical purposes it is virtually useless. Even if this were true—we shall have to consider later on how far it is true—it is essential to appreciate the importance of this conception historically. When Aquinas propounded his system of moral theology, it was based fundamentally on this conception of Natural Law; for it was this and nothing else which made it possible for him to accept the Aristotelian conception of ethics and politics and adapt it to the purposes of Christian theology. It is not surprising that many in his time regarded him as a dangerous modernist. Nevertheless, he won the battle and

[1] *Ibid.* Q. 94 a. 4 and a. 6.

for many centuries—indeed, up to this very day in many quarters—Moral Theology has stood foursquare upon this foundation.

The reason for the ultimate victory of Thomistic ethics and moral theology is doubtless in large part due to the fact that Christianity sprang from the Old Testament and that the Decalogue of necessity had an important influence upon it. Aquinas argues that the Old Testament Law was essentially good, inasmuch as, like the Natural Law, it was agreeable to reason. He mentions in particular its prohibition of lust or greed in the Tenth Commandment, since lust in any form is contrary to the dictates of reason. Moreover, he is able to appeal to the evidence of St. Paul who, despite his criticism of the Jewish Law does not hesitate to call it 'good' (Rom. 7. 16). When he passes to the New Testament he speaks of it as the New Law, without raising any question as to the propriety of this. Again, he is able to appeal to certain expressions in the Pauline epistles. Thus he quotes the Apostle as speaking of 'the law of faith' (Rom. 3. 27) and he points to the remarkable expression which occurs later in the same epistle, 'the law of the Spirit of life in Christ Jesus' (Rom. 8. 2). He rather surprisingly makes no reference to all that might be set on the other side in the New Testament—evidence to which we shall later have to turn our attention. It seems to be enough for him that the new law is a law of grace. The New Law, he argues, possesses two characteristics. First and foremost the inner grace of the Holy Spirit is bestowed by it; and by this grace man is justified. In the second place, however, there are the ordinances and moral commands of the New Covenant, and by these man stands condemned, so that if any man deliberately sins after receiving the grace of the New Law he is worthy of greater condemnation, as being ungrateful for the greater blessings he enjoys and failing to use the grace given to him, which is sufficient for his needs.

But it is the same God who gave both laws. The Old Law was written in stone; the New Law was written in the fleshly tables of the heart.[1] But, according to Aquinas, it was still 'a law,' i.e. an external authoritative standard of conduct. There seems to be no question in his mind about this; there is no suggestion that because Christianity is a 'religion of the Spirit' it is therefore not also based upon an authoritative moral law—fully as authoritative as the Law of Moses.

Ever since the time of Aquinas, therefore, moral theology has been based on law. It has been assumed, rather than argued, that this is the only approach. Thus, for example, Lehmkuhl asserts 'without law conscience would lack a foundation and be deprived of its proper power to bind.'[2] Or again, Koch-Preuss says: 'Law, therefore, is but another name for the divine will recognized as the standard of human conduct.'[3] Again, Slater says of the judgements of conscience: 'The major premise will be some general law of conduct.'[4] It is needless to multiply examples. Roman Catholic moralists, to a man, base their moral theology on a legal foundation, and have done so ever since Aquinas.

This legal basis has determined the shape of casuistry in Western moral theology. Casuistry is very far from being the whole of moral theology, but it is certainly an important part of it; and the fact that the claims of morality are always conceived strictly in terms of law makes it possible, and indeed necessary, for law and liberty to stand over against one another as rival claimants. Hence the importance of the maxim: *In dubio melior est conditio possidentis*. In other words, possession is nine points of the law. The position is clearly set out by Slater in the following passage: 'Possession is properly a physical fact, and consists in the corporal retention

---

[1] *Ibid.* Q. 106 a. 2.   [2] A. Lehmkuhl: *Theologia Moralis*, Vol. I, p. 55.
[3] Koch-Preuss: *Handbook of Moral Theology*, Vol. I, p. 120.
[4] T. Slater: *A Manual of Moral Theology*, Vol. I, p. 29.

of a thing. In a wider sense rights are objects of possession, as a right of way, or the right to one's liberty; so that if one's liberty has hitherto been unrestricted, it is said to be in possession. The very fact of possession gives a right to continue in possession unless there is an adverse and stronger claim. There is also in the possessor a presumption of title to possess, for all men are jealous of their rights, and usually do not allow their property or rights to be held by others as owners. If, then, I am in possession of some object or right, and a doubt supervenes as to whether I am entitled to possession in the case or not, the question may be solved in the forum of conscience as it would be in a court of law, by applying the maxim—*in dubio melior est conditio possidentis.* If, then, a doubt arises as to whether I have said my breviary, I must say it, for the law is in possession; if on the contrary a doubt comes into my mind as to whether I have taken food after midnight, I may go to Holy Communion, because my right to receive is in possession.'

It cannot be denied that in this kind of casuistry there is a balm for scrupulous consciences, and it cannot be denied that it is an important part of the task of casuistry to ease such consciences. A scrupulous person who has been taught to adopt this approach, or who has the help of a director who does so, has a great advantage over any other kind of scrupulous person, who may well be tortured by his or her scruples to such an extent that life becomes a perpetual 'dither.' We might parody a remark of St. Paul's made in another connexion: 'It is better to be lax than to dither.' We have also to remember that before a doubt can come before the tribunal of casuistry, it has to be a serious doubt. In the examples given by Slater the doubt concerns a point of fact in each case; but of course the doubt may concern not a point of fact but a point of law. For example, one who has been brought up to regard the drinking of alcoholic beverages as sinful may begin to doubt whether in fact it is sinful;

or, contrariwise, one who has been brought up to drink alcoholic liquors may begin to wonder if, in fact, it is legitimate, and be seriously troubled by his doubts in the light of a tragic instance of alcohol leading to the break-up of a marriage. The legal approach to this problem means that the former should continue to be teetotal until his doubts are solved, whereas the latter can go on drinking until his doubts are resolved. In the former case, law is in possession, but in the latter, liberty is in possession.

To the minds of some, however, this approach seems to be too 'slick' and rule of thumb. Moreover, it is certainly the case that it is not always satisfactory to state our moral problems in this form. The question is often that of determining where our duty lies—e.g. in the matter of almsgiving. How much should I give to this good cause? How much should I give week by week to the Church? How much should I allow myself to spend on what are called luxuries? It is difficult, if not impossible, to solve such doubts as these by means of the traditional approach.[1]

It is fair to say that part of the strength of the traditional approach to moral theology in general and to casuistry in particular lies in the fact that it is of great value to two classes of persons, and, indeed, for one of them, the only possible line of approach. The first of these classes is the clergy in their dealing with penitents, though even here caution is required lest law degenerates into legalism. The second class of persons is the scrupulous. For such the legal approach is the only possible road to deliver them from the frustration and even the paralysis of perpetual doubt. On the other hand, it also has great weaknesses, and these were particularly evident to the Reformers, to whom we must now turn.

---

[1] It is significant that Aquinas in his full discussion of the question of almsgiving (S.T. IIa–IIae. Q. 32) makes no attempt to face this question.

CHAPTER 2

THE REFORMATION AND POST-REFORMATION APPROACH

BOTH Luther and Calvin, though in different ways, undermined the significance of Natural Law. Luther's general attitude to natural law—I say 'general' because he was not a systematic or consistent writer—is well exemplified in the Preface to his translation into German of the Old Testament. He sees clearly that in the Old Testament a great deal of attention is paid to law where the divine law of the old covenant is fully set forth. The reason for this, according to Luther, is that the mind of man has been so darkened by sin that he is quite incapable of understanding God's law. 'Where God's law (i.e. Revealed Law) is not, there human reason is so blind that it cannot recognize sin. Human reason does not know that unbelief and despair of God is sin; nay it knows nothing about man's duty to believe God and trust Him; thus it goes on hardened in its blindness, and feels this sin not at all, doing meanwhile some works that would otherwise be good and leading an outwardly honourable life. Then it thinks it stands well, and enough has been done in this matter. We see this in the heathen and the hypocrites, when their life is at its best. Besides, the reason does not know that the wicked inclination of the flesh and hatred against enemies are sin, but because it feels that all men are so inclined, it holds that these things are natural and right and thinks it enough to guard against outward wrongdoing. Thus it goes on and regards its illness as strength, its sin as right, its bad as good, and can make no progress.'[1] Consequently the law of Moses is necessary to remove the scales from men's eyes. But it

[1] *Preface to the Old Testament*: E.T. Philadelphia Edition, Vol. 6, p. 374.

goes further than this. It makes to be sins actions which are no sins—such as eating leavened bread at the Passover or eating unclean food—in order to heap sin upon sin and to bring men to realize the exceeding sinfulness of sin and to become aware of the need of grace. All that is required in fact is faith and love, and therefore any law which conflicts with that—even those prohibiting murder or adultery— see the case of the son of the widow of Tekoa who killed his brother (2 *Sam.* 14. 11) or the marriage of Tamar (1 *Sam.* 21. 6)—can be set aside.

Similar teaching is given by Luther in his *Treatise on Good Works* in the section dealing with the First Commandment. He writes: 'You might say: "Why do we have so many laws of the Church and of the State, and many ceremonies of churches, monastic houses, holy places, which urge and tempt men to good works, if faith does all things through the first commandment?" I answer: simply because we do not all have faith or do not heed it. If every man had faith, we would need no more laws, but every one would of himself at all times do good works, as his confidence in God teaches him.'[1] Thus Luther does not so much deny the existence of the Natural Law—at times he can appeal to it[2]— as evacuate it of its true meaning.

In general, therefore, it may be said that for Luther the conception of Natural Law, as understood previously, becomes inoperative, and moral theology unnecessary. If the moral life of Christians is based entirely on justification by faith, it follows that faith must be all that is required. Since, moreover, it comes through the hearing of the Word of God there can be no question of its being the supernatural crowning and completion of what is operative in every man.

[1] *Treatise on Good Works. Ibid.* Vol. 1, p. 199.
[2] See e.g. the story of Charles the Bold which he recorded in *Secular Authority: To What Extent it should be Obeyed. Ibid.* Vol. 3, p. 273. See also his *Exposition of the Decalogue.*

Troeltsch is not far wrong[1] when he says that Lutheranism misrepresented the natural forms of life (previously guaranteed by Natural Law doctrine), which are autonomous and must be so, by regarding them merely as a field for the exercise of Christian love individualistically conceived; it is solely out of love that the Christian submits to community life at all.

When we pass to Calvin, we find that for him also Natural Law has little significance. He acknowledges its existence, but owing to the sin of man the light which it brings is all but extinguished. In fact, its only purpose is that it may deprive man of any excuse for his sin. He says roundly in the *Institutes*: 'The end of Natural Law is to render man inexcusable.'[2] In his commentary on Romans 2. 14, 15 Calvin writes: 'There are naturally grafted in the minds of all men certain conceptions of justice and uprightness, which the Greeks call *prolepseis*, cogitations or devices. They have, therefore, a law without the Law, because, though they have not the written law of Moses, yet they are not altogether void of the knowledge of right and equity; for otherwise they could not distinguish between vice and virtue.' Calvin here agrees with Luther that the function of the Jewish Law was to unfilm the eye and make it possible for man to perceive what his blindness had previously prevented him from seeing. In his commentary on Psalm 19 he brings this out, reiterating the teaching of the *Institutes* that the function of the Natural Law is that man might be 'without excuse.' He writes: 'While the heavens bear witness concerning God, their testimony does not lead men so far that they thereby learn truly to fear him, and acquire a well-grounded knowledge of him; it serves only to render them inexcusable. It is doubtless true, that if we were not very dull and stupid, the signs and proofs of God

[1] See Troeltsch: *The Social Teaching of the Christian Churches*, pp. 540, 543.
[2] Book II, 22.

which are to be found on the earthly scene are abundant
enough to lead us to acknowledge and reverence him, but
since, though surrounded with so clear a light, we are still
blind, this wonderful revelation of the glory of God,
without the aid of the Word, would profit us nothing,
although it should be to us a loud and distinct proclamation
sounding in our ears.'[1]

There is another strain in Calvin's teaching which makes
it impossible for him to do justice to the idea of Natural
Law and that is his doctrine of the absolute Sovereignty of
God, which is, indeed, the basis of the whole structure of
his thought. Professor Entrèves says in this connexion: 'The
similarity between Calvin's notion of God as *legibus solutus*
and the modern conception of sovereignty is a fascinating
subject for research and reflection. The analogy has been
pointed out many times, and attention has been called to
Calvin's early training in the law as a possible source of his
notion of God's sovereignty. . . . Protestantism did not lead
necessarily to a complete break with the old tradition of
natural law. The impact of the Reformation upon the
continuity of legal political thought is still the subject of
controversy among scholars. But it seems obvious enough
that the Thomist conception of natural law, as a mediatory
element between God and man, and as an assertion of the
power and dignity of human nature, would have been out
of place in the Reformers' theology, and actually they
found little or no room for it.'[2]

Thus it is clear that the traditional approach to questions
of moral theology was abandoned by the earliest reformers.
Indeed, they left little room for it in their scheme of things.
So far as Calvin is concerned, M. Benoit has written an
interesting book in which he reveals to us the Reformer as

[1] *Commentary on Psalm* 19.
[2] A. P. Entrèves: *Natural Law* (1951), pp. 69 and 70.

a director of souls.[1] We see him dealing with various moral questions—such as the attitude which those of the reformed religion should adopt towards Roman Catholicism, the binding force of vows, the possibility of legitimate lying, and problems of marriage. We see here that Calvin hovers strangely as a director between extreme rigorism and laxity. When it comes to dealings with Romanism no compromise is possible. Thus he writes to one who holds high office under the French crown who wants to know if it is legitimate for him to accompany his Sovereign to church when required to do so, and tells him that rather than have anything to do with this idolatry he should risk dismissal. Even the Scriptural precedent of Naaman being permitted to 'bow down in the house of Rimmon' is considered inadequate.[2] On the other hand, a wife who had given a solemn promise to her husband on his death-bed that she would not have anything to do with Calvin and his teaching is 'absolved' of her promise in view of the fact that Papalism is utterly idolatrous. All is fair in dealing with idolatry. Such moral guidance, in fact, follows naturally upon a doctrine which ascribes absolute sovereignty to God. It is, however, not to be dignified with the name of moral theology.

The Lutheran and Calvinistic attitude towards the idea of law has become even more negative in the writings of modern continental Protestants. One of the foremost modern Protestant treatises on ethics, Brunner's *The Divine Imperative*, for example, clearly shows this. No distinction is drawn between law and 'legalism,' which is regarded as the chief enemy. Goodness is not to be found enshrined in any set of moral laws or principles, but only in obedience to God. 'This obedience,' writes Brunner, 'is rendered not to a law or a principle which can be known beforehand, but

---

[1] Jean-Daniel Benoit: *Calvin, Directeur D'Ames* (1944).   [2] *Op. cit.*, p. 229.

only to the free, sovereign will of God.'[1] Here we have the Calvinistic doctrine of God as *legibus solutus*, with all the evil consequences which follow from it.

On the other side, Brunner does less than justice to the traditional position which he opposes. He says: 'In this explicit rejection of the legalistic definition of the Good the truly Christian ethic is also distinguished from the Roman Catholic [*sic*] ethic. In accordance with its juridically defined conception of faith and of the Church its conception of the Good is also rigidly legalistic, and therefore its ethical system is fundamentally a system of casuistry. The lesser stipulations are logically derived from the universal law, and by means of a closely woven network of further minor regulations the whole realm of human life is legally defined so that for every case, in actual practice, it is possible to look up the ethical code and find out what is commanded and what is forbidden.'[2] It is surprising that a responsible theologian can commit himself to such a parody of the position which he is opposing; but at least he is entirely correct when he goes on to say that 'this conception cannot be combined with the knowledge of justification by faith alone.' This latter means that faith is all that is required for the living of the Christian life, faith that works by love. There is, indeed, a place for moral laws—the Decalogue, for instance—but these are only for the unbeliever. The true believer, *in so far as* he is a believer, breaks through these laws. 'Just as the bud breaks through its sheath, so the believing obedience of love must break through the law from within. The law, both in the sense of "laws which stand written," and in the sense of the law which is written on our conscience, is the husk within which God means the fruit of faith to ripen. But, as we have already seen, when the fruit is ripe, the outer covering must be actually *broken*.'[3] It is obvious that there is no place for

---

[1] E. Brunner: *The Divine Imperative* (E.T.), p. 83.   [2] *Op. cit.*, p. 91.
[3] *Ibid.*, p. 143.

moral theology here. *Dilige et fac quod vis* is a sufficient maxim to replace it.

It was the Caroline theologians, Robert Sanderson and Jeremy Taylor, who first sought to reform traditional moral theology instead of doing away with it. Dr. McAdoo rightly says: 'In a real sense, the Carolines are the true successors of St. Thomas.'[1] We turn, therefore, to a brief account of Sanderson's moral theology.

Sanderson adopts the traditional approach, although he is extremely critical of the Roman Catholic Church. Indeed, in this he departs from the judicious attitude of mind which is usually so characteristic of him, and is less than fair in his criticisms. Nevertheless, he does not lose his head. He does not conclude, as the earliest reformers had done, that the whole inherited system of thought based on law must be jettisoned. On the contrary, he sees that in some form it is indispensable, and he sets himself carefully to separate the precious from the vile. In his justly famous *Lectures on Conscience and Law*, in discussing the rule of conscience he begins by laying it down 'that conscience can never exercise her office as she ought, unless some rules are established, by which she is to be obliged; for wherever there is an active virtue wholly undetermined in its own nature, and able to act well or ill . . . it is necessary that there should be some rule or law to govern and direct its actions.'[2] He proceeds to say that there are four degrees of moral obligation. First and foremost, stands that which God commands. He is speaking in this lecture from the passage in St. James 4. 12: 'For there is one Lawgiver, who is able to save and destroy.' All law, therefore, ultimately is based upon the Divine Will. In the second place stands human law. In the third, laws with which we bind ourselves by vows and oaths. Finally, we have laws which bind the conscience

[1] H. R. McAdoo: *The Structure of Caroline Moral Theology* (1949), p. 31.
[2] *Lectures on Conscience and Human Law*, ed. Wordsworth (1877), p. 88.

accidentally, in order to avoid giving scandal or offence to others. He follows the traditional teaching concerning Natural Law, the basic principle of which is that Good is to be done, and Evil avoided. Sanderson points out that there are secondary precepts which follow upon this, such as that parents are to be honoured, children brought up, our neighbour's life to be preserved, pledges to be restored, and so forth. The laws of the Decalogue, he argues, are binding on Christians only in so far as they embody the natural law, or as they are endorsed by our Lord.

All this traditional thought Sanderson takes over, but he gives it a new direction. It is clear that ultimately the authority of the individual conscience must stand, but it does not follow that law must be abolished in order to establish human freedom. 'Both these Laws,' Sanderson writes, 'the Old Law of Moses in general, and the New Law of Christ, as far as morality is concerned, are exploded by the Antinomians, Anabaptists, Enthusiasts, of our own times and by the rest of that portentous crew, as useless: and (when a Christian is come to full maturity in Christ, and is anointed with the unction of the Spirit) as unworthy of his care and attention. These men acknowledge no Law but the Law of Faith, and the dictates of the Spirit. I have no time to confute these Sectaries, nor have I much occasion, since the Apostle St. James has so directly struck at the root of these monstrous errors, as if, by a prophetic spirit, he had designed of set purpose to refute them.'[1]

Sanderson, then, is quite clear about the necessity of Law; but he will have nothing to do with legalism, and it is here that we see him striking out a new line towards a revised and reformed moral theology. He takes a grave view of sin. He writes: 'We use to teach, and that truly, according to the plain evidence of Scripture and the judgement of the ancient Fathers, against the contrary tenet of the later

[1] *Ibid.* § 27, p. 112.

Church of Rome, that all the works of unbelievers and natural men are not only stained with sin, for so are the best works of the faithful too, but also are really and truly sins, because they spring from a corrupt fountain, for "that which is born of the flesh is flesh." . . . St. Augustine's judgement concerning such works is well known, who pronounceth of the best of them, that they are but *splendida peccata*; and the best of them are indeed no better. . . . For the whole man being corrupted through the fall of Adam, the conscience also is wrapped in the common pollution, so that "to them that are defiled and unbelieving nothing is pure, but even their mind and conscience is defiled," as speaketh St. Paul.'[1] But he can go on, in the next breath, to eulogize those among the unregenerate who were ready to suffer for the sake of a good conscience. Not having the Law, they were, as St. Paul says, a law unto themselves 'choosing rather to undergo the greatest miseries, shame and torment, exile, yea, death itself, or any thing that could befall them, than wilfully to transgress those rules and notions, and dictates of piety and equity, which the God of Nature had imprinted in their consciences.'[2] It is perhaps a little difficult to equate this with what Sanderson had earlier in the same discourse called 'the glimmering light of depraved nature' and 'that spark of the light of nature which was in them.' But at any rate the dimmer the light which they followed, the nobler their conduct seems to be. One thing emerges clearly from what Sanderson has to say about all this, and that is his unwillingness to have anything to do with Pelagianism in any shape or form. Legalism is absolutely excluded.

The same holds good of Laxism. Sanderson, like most of the Caroline divines, leans well over in the direction of a Rigoristic or Tutiorist casuistry. This comes out most plainly when he discusses the question of a choice between two evils. 'But what? will some reply: In case two sins be

---

[1] *Sermon ad Populum,* § 23 Works, Vol. III, p. 235.   [2] *Ibid.* § 24, p. 237.

propounded, may I not do the lesser, to avoid the greater? Otherwise must I not of necessity do the greater? The answer is short and easy. If two sins be propounded, do neither. *E malis minimum* holdeth, as you heard (and not always neither), in evils of pain. But that is no rule for evils of sin. Here the safer rule is, *E malis nullum.* . . . But what if both cannot be avoided, but that one must needs be done? In such a strait may I not choose the lesser? To thee, I say again, Choose neither.'[1] There is however, an insuperable objecton to this position, and that is that cases arise in which inaction involves making a choice. Such is the case in the well-known dilemma of the surgeon who has to choose between saving the life of the mother or the baby. If he operates, he will cause the death of the child; if he docs nothing, he will cause the death of the mother. In either case, he is a killer. Apart from this, tutiorism in any form is unworkable, and in the face of scrupulous consciences is disastrous. The only advice which Sanderson can give to those afflicted with scruples is: 'It behoveth every man, first, to be wary that he do not at all admit them, if he can choose: or if he cannot wholly avoid them, that, secondly, he endeavour so far as may be to eject them speedily out of his thoughts, as Satan's snares, and things that may breed him worser inconveniences: or, if he cannot be so rid of them, that then, thirdly, he resolve to go according to the more probable persuasion of his mind, and despise these scruples.'[2] Here he descends to Probabiliorism, which, so far as the scrupulous is concerned, is all one with Tutiorism. In all this doubtless we see the influence of reaction against the laxism of some Roman Catholic moralists—an influence which can be discerned in the case of nearly all the Caroline theologians, but which, although unfortunate, must not

[1] Sermon II, *ad clerum*, §§ 25 and 26 Works, Vol. II, p. 61.
[2] Sermon IV, *ad clerum*, § 33, *Ibid.*, p. 139.

blind us to the great work which they did in the revival of moral theology.

The greatness of Sanderson in moral theology consists chiefly in three points. First, he is a pioneer in reforming moral theology. Holding fast to traditional principles as found in his master, Aquinas, he does not follow them slavishly. In particular he restores the individual conscience to its rightful place in opposition to the over-authoritarianism of the Papacy—which he calls (rather unfairly) 'the tyranny of the Roman Pontiff.'[1] Secondly, and on the other hand, he sees the great dangers of individualism and insists that 'due regard may be paid to the authority of the Catholic Church, and to the judgement of men of piety and learning.'[2] Thirdly, his keen and clear mind enables him to treat the most complex moral problems with extreme lucidity, which rightly gained for him his great reputation as a master of casuistry.

Contemporary with Sanderson was Jeremy Taylor, who was born some twenty years after Sanderson but died only four years after him, thus having a much shorter span of life. It is one of the peculiarities of history that these two great men—perhaps the greatest of all English moral theologians—should have overlapped. It is one of the tragedies of history that they seem to have had so little in common and worked independently, or largely independently. They were both royal chaplains and we know that they met at times in their attendance upon the king,[3] but unfortunately they fell out over the question of original sin—Taylor favouring a milder doctrine than Sanderson—and this drove them finally apart. Taylor's chief work of moral theology, *Ductor Dubitantium*, was published in 1657, the same year as Sanderson published his Lectures on law and conscience.

[1] *Lectures on Conscience and Human Law*, Lecture III, § 28, p. 84.
[2] *Ibid.*, § 31, p. 86.
[3] See the reference to this in his letter to Thomas Barlow. Works, Vol. VI, p. 386.

But the lectures themselves had been delivered twelve years earlier, and it is hard to think that Taylor was unaware of them. Yet he makes no reference to them or to Sanderson, and in the Preface to *Ductor Dubitantium* he implies that he is the pioneer in reforming the study of moral theology, which was less than the truth. He writes: 'It is a great work and too heavy for one man's shoulders; but somebody must begin; and yet no man ever would, if he can be affrighted with the consideration of any difficulty in the world. But I have laid aside all considerations of myself, and with entire dependence upon God for help, I have begun an institution of moral theology, and established it upon such principles and instruments of probation which every man allows, and better than which we have none imparted to us. I affirm nothing but upon grounds of Scripture, or universal tradition, or right reason discernible by every disinterested person, where the questions are of great concern, and can admit of these probations: where they cannot, I take the next best: the laws of wise commonwealths and the sayings of wise men, the results of fame and the proverbs of the ancients, the precedents of holy persons and the great examples of saints.'[1] Later on he continues: '1. In hard and intricate questions I take that which is easy and intelligible, and concerning which it will be easy to judge whether it be right or wrong. 2. In odious things and matters of burden and envy, I take that part which is least, unless there be evident reason to the contrary. 3. In favours I always choose the largest sense, when anyone is bettered by that sense, and no man is the worse. 4. In things and questions relating to men, I give those answers that take away scruples, and bring peace and a quiet mind. 5. In things relating to God, I always choose to speak that thing which to him is most honourable. 6. In matters of duty, I always choose that which is most holy. 7. In doubts I choose what is safest. 8. In probabilities I

---

[1] *Ductor Dubitantium*, Preface. Works, ed. Heber, Vol. XI, p. 356.

C

prefer that which is the more reasonable, never allowing to anyone a leave of choosing that which is confessedly the less reasonable in the whole conjunction of circumstances and relative considerations.'[1] He concludes by saying: 'He that endeavours to keep a good conscience and an honest mind, besides that he will inquire after his duty sufficiently, he will be able to tell very much of it himself; for God will assist him, and cause that "his own mind shall tell him more than seven watchmen that sit in a tower"; and if he miss, he is next to an excuse, and God is ready to pardon him.'[2]

In this summary of his guiding principles we find much common ground between Sanderson and himself. We see the same reliance upon reason and Holy Scripture, the same emphasis upon the importance of the individual conscience, the same tendency towards tutiorism. But when Taylor proceeds to develop his theme he is markedly inferior to Sanderson in lucidity and grasp. His work is characterized by a prolixity that is almost pathological and compares unfavourably with Sanderson's clear-cut treatment of law. As we have seen, the latter follows Aquinas pretty closely in dealing with this matter and especially with Natural Law, as Hooker had done in his majestic treatment of this theme in the first Book of the *Ecclesiastical Polity*. Taylor's treatment is confused. He misrepresents Aquinas in saying that he teaches that natural law is that which man has in common with the beasts.[3] That, for St. Thomas, is only the lowest grade of the law of nature and not characteristic of it as found in man. And when he goes on to say that 'All the laws of Christ concerning moral actions are the laws of nature'[4] he makes a serious confusion between nature and super-nature.

There is one point of particular importance not only for the appreciation of Taylor's moral theology, but also for the

[1] *Ibid.*, pp. 358 and 359.   [2] *Ibid.*, p. 367.   [3] *Op. cit.*, Vol. XII, p. 196.
[4] *Ibid.*, p. 227.

understanding of the Caroline reformation as a whole, and that is his dislike of the distinction between mortal and venial sin. In this he is at one with Sanderson,[1] but the latter does not develop the objections which can be raised, as Taylor does in his other chief work on moral theology, *Unum Necessarium*. Bishop Kirk once rightly pointed out that the chief value of this distinction is not for the penitent but for the confessor and director. The fact that the Carolines generally cannot see any good in this distinction shows how much they were concerned to enlarge the field of moral theology to include far more than the confessional. They were concerned, in fact, as far as possible to make every man his own casuist; and from this point of view the distinction between mortal and venial sin is of more than doubtful value.

Taylor puts forward four main objections to this distinction, and he quotes St. Basil with approval as saying that the New Testament knows nothing of it. It is surprising that nothing is said here about the distinction in the First Epistle of St. John between 'a sin unto death' and 'a sin not unto death.'[2] In the first place, Taylor admits that a distinction can rightly be drawn between greater and lesser sins, and he quotes most of the relevant New Testament passages which support this. He says: 'He is a greater criminal that steals the chalice from a church than he that takes a few coleworts, or robs a garden of cucumbers. . . . But this, when it is reduced to its proper cause, is, because such greater sins are complicated; they are commonly two or three sins wrapped together, as the unchastity of a priest, is uncleanness and scandal too; adultery is worse than fornication, because it is unchastity and injustice.'[3] We cannot, therefore, use this evidence to support the distinction between mortal and venial.

---

[1] *De Juramenti Obligatione* III. 15 Works, Vol. IV, p. 283.
[2] 1 John 5. 16.   [3] *Op. cit.*, Vol. VIII, p. 339.

Secondly, no sin is *per se* venial. No man can love sin and love God at the same time. In order to understand this point 'we must distinguish the formal from the material part. The formality of sin is disobedience to God, and turning from him to the creature by love and adhesion. The material part is the action itself. The first can never happen without our will; but the latter may by surprise, and indeliberation, and imperfection of condition. For in this life our understanding is weak, our attention trifling, our advertency interrupted, our diversions many, our divisions of spirit irresistible, our knowledge little, our dullness frequent, our mistakes many, our fears potent, and betrayers of our reason; and at any one of these doors sin may enter, in its material part, while the will is inactive, or the understanding dull, or the affections busy, or the spirit otherwise employed, or the faculties wearied, or reason abused; therefore if you inquire for venial sins, they must be in this throng of imperfections, but they never go higher. Let no man therefore say I have a desire to please myself in some little things; for if he desires it he may not do it, that very desire makes that it cannot be venial, but as damnable as any, in its proportion.'[1]

Thirdly, no man must dare to measure his own sin, 'because it being his own case he is an unequal and incompetent judge; his temptation is his prejudice and his bribe, and it is ten to one he will suck in the poison, by his making himself believe that the potion is not deadly.'[2] It is for God alone, Taylor says, to assess the greater or less in sin.

The fourth and final objection to the distinction between mortal and venial is that by giving heed to this 'men are taught to arrest their repentances, and have leave not to proceed farther.'[3] He sums up: 'A man may be choked with a raisin, as well as with great morsels of flesh; and a small leak in a ship, if it be neglected, will as certainly sink her as

<hr>

[1] *Ibid.*, p. 367.   [2] *Ibid.*, p. 376.   [3] *Ibid.*, p. 364.

if she sprang a plank. Death is the wages of all; and damnation is the portion of the impenitent, whatever was the instance of their sin.'[1] In all this we see Taylor at his best as a moralist. He makes his readers realize that moral theology cannot be divorced from ascetic theology, and that, rightly understood, it is concerned all the time to lead men to God.

[1] *Ibid.*, p. 383.

CHAPTER 3

THE MODERN APPROACH

WE have seen that the great Caroline moralists, Sanderson and Taylor, continued the traditional approach to moral theology by way of law, while at the same time they eschewed legalism. They do not quote authorities or draw up lists of cases. Their appeal is to reason and Holy Scripture. They are as much concerned with the individual soul when he is outside the confessional as when he is inside. They dislike the post-Tridentine separation between moral and ascetical theology. They maintain that moral theology is primarily concerned not with sustaining a minimum standard of Christian behaviour but with leading men to perfection. Hence they will have nothing to do with the distinction between mortal and venial sin and in their casuistry they lean overmuch towards rigorism. In most of this it can be truly said they are progressive, and that they gave a lead for future moral theologians. It is, therefore, all the more unfortunate that their lead was not followed. Soon after their death the Church of England entered upon the dry and barren period of one hundred and fifty years or more when Methodism was almost the only spiritual force in the land. Moreover, when the Oxford Movement took its rise, and attention was once more turned to the problems of moral theology, their work was neglected. This was doubtless due to the fact that it had been set out in anything but a popular form. Sanderson's chief work was in Latin, and Jeremy Taylor's *Ductor Dubitantium*, although indeed written in English, was so diffuse and, on the whole, so dull that it was allowed to remain unread on the dusty shelves of libraries. Those who sought to revive the study of moral theology did what Jeremy Taylor described (rather harshly) as going 'down to the forges of the Philistines to sharpen every man his share and his coulter, his axe and his mattock.'[1] It is, for example, most significant that in one of the earliest books written on this subject by an Anglican in this century, Belton's *Manual for Confessors*—which has been invaluable to very many of the clergy—neither Sanderson nor Jeremy Taylor appears in the list of authors in the bibliography. Belton wrote: 'To our shame, it must be confessed that an Anglican text-book on Moral Theology has yet to be written—that is, a book in which the subject of morals is treated in a thoroughly scientific manner. That such a book will have to be written does not admit of any doubt, but in the meantime the only thing we can do is to study books on Moral Theology approved by Roman Catholic authors, despite the not entirely unjust prejudice some people feel against using them.'[2] It might seem that he had never opened the works of the Caroline moralists.

Such, then, was the position of moral theology at the opening of the present century so far as the English Church is concerned. Between then and now a valiant attempt to revive an interest in the subject was made by Bishop Kirk— an attempt which has met with a considerable amount of success. But we still await anything approaching an Anglican text-book of moral theology; and indeed perhaps the time is not ripe for it. Before that can come into existence, it will probably be necessary to explore fully the possibilities of a more empirical approach to the subject. We live in a scientific age, and even the 'reformation' initiated by Sanderson and Taylor preceded the rise of modern experimental science. It is not surprising, therefore, that our younger theological moralists are pleading for a more empirical approach to the subject. For example, Canon

---

[1] Taylor: *Ductor Dubitantium*, Preface, Works, Vol. XI, p. 346.
[2] F. G. Belton: *Manual for Confessors* (1916), p. 114.

R. H. Preston, writing in *Theology* in January 1961, criticized
the whole accustomed approach to moral theology, saying:
'There is too much law in it, too many hair-splitting legal
distinctions, too much deduction from fixed principles, too
little attention to empirical evidence (for instance in psychology and sociology), too simple a notion of the term
"natural," and too little concern for perfection as against
minimum obligations.'

Our brief examination of the work of Sanderson and
Taylor is sufficient to show that a good many of these
criticisms are not valid as against their standpoint. We
certainly do not find in their writings 'hair-splitting legal
distinctions' or 'too little concern for perfection.' Nor, on
the whole, is it fair to say that they are guilty of 'too much
deduction from fixed principles.' But it is true that they
adopt the *a priori* rather than the empirical approach; and
it is at this point that the modern approach will part company with them. To what extent this is the case it is now our
purpose to inquire.

We must begin by considering briefly the general approach
to moral problems which characterizes the New Testament.
It is a commonplace to say that the New Testament is rooted
in the Old, and, despite the arguments of some writers, it
may be said to be generally agreed that it cannot really be
understood if this is forgotten. Now it is indisputable that
the morality of the Old Testament rests upon the conception
of Law. It is based on the Decalogue, which is understood
as being a set of commands given from on high. There is
nothing empirical here! This Law of Moses was common
ground as between our Lord and his hearers. He did not
seek to abolish it. On the contrary, he claimed to fulfil it.
By this he apparently meant that it was his intention to
bring out its full meaning. He did this by re-interpreting
the first nine Commandments in terms of the tenth. The
tenth Commandment is the only one which is concerned

directly with men's thoughts: 'Thou shalt not covet.' Our
Lord shows that the other commandments can only really
be fully observed if they are interpreted internally. Thus
the commandment against murder becomes a commandment against the harbouring of murderous thoughts of
hatred. The commandment against adultery becomes a
command against the harbouring of adulterous thoughts.
The commandment to observe the Sabbath Day in like
manner can only be kept if the inner meaning of the Sabbath
is borne in mind. 'The Sabbath was made for man and not
man for the Sabbath.' This point is sometimes put by saying
that the Christian must keep the Commandments in the
spirit rather than in the letter. This statement of the case,
however, is liable to misunderstanding; for it must not be
taken to mean—as it is sometimes taken—that the letter
does not have to be kept at all.

This reinterpretation of the Decalogue which our Lord
puts forward is in line with the earlier reinterpretation which
was made by the author of the Book of Deuteronomy.
This reinterpretation is given by the latter by means of the
word 'love' (*ahabha*). As S. R. Driver says: 'The *love* of
God . . . is set forth in Deuteronomy as the fundamental
motive of human action.'[1] This momentous reinterpretation
of the Decalogue was adopted by our Lord and made central
in his moral teaching, insomuch that, in Greek, what was
virtually a new word (*agape*) was coined in order to achieve
this.

In this way the moral Law was internalized, and the
danger of legalism was minimized, yet it remains true to
say that the legal approach was not abandoned entirely.
Moral conduct still means conformity with the will of God
and obedience to his commands. The crucial question is:
How is the moral law to be interpreted? Or, to put the
question in another way: How is man to discover where his

[1] *Commentary on Deuteronomy*, I.C.C., *ad loc.*, p. 91.

duty lies? The obvious answer which the Christian, instructed by the New Testament, will give, is: By the guidance of the Holy Spirit. This is the uniform teaching of the New Testament. But this raises a further question which, unfortunately, is not always asked: How is this guidance given? Is it given primarily to the Christian Community as a whole, i.e. to the Church, or is it given primarily to the individual? There are few more important moral questions than that. It is probably true to say that the average Christian in this country would say in reply to this question: This guidance is given to each individual. Yet when the New Testament is carefully studied, it is doubtful if this is the tenor of its teaching. The fact of the matter is that the ingrained individualism of so much of our English thinking leads us to read this into the NewTestament rather than out of it. It is this which causes us to read 'You' as second person singular instead of second person plural whenever we meet it in the New Testament; and yet in almost every case it is the latter.

In the account of the descent of the Holy Spirit at Pentecost in Acts 2, it is clear that we have the description of an experience which is both corporate and individual. The Holy Spirit like fire welded the disciples into a *Koinonia*, but the tongues as of fire sat upon each of them. But as the story of the infant Christian Church proceeds it is clear enough that we have nothing like the unbridled individualism which has been read into it. On the contrary, wherever this breaks out, it is rebuked. All things must be done decently and in order. Disputes must be settled by the Holy Spirit speaking to the whole Church through the Apostles in the Council of Jerusalem. The individualistic schismatical spirit which leads individuals to exclaim 'I am of Paul and I am of Apollos' is severely rebuked. Christian Love is evidently not the purely individualistic conception which some modern writers often take it to be.

It seems to be clear that, if we are to do justice to the New Testament moral teaching, we must take the corporate nature of the Christian religion really seriously—far more seriously than most of us are prepared to do. Christian theology and Christian conduct alike depend upon the community. Dr. W. G. Pollard in his interesting book, *Physicist and Christian*, has argued forcibly that all true knowledge must be based on membership in a community. He illustrates his thesis from his own experience as a physicist. He points out that the common idea that scientific knowledge, being abstract, is not in any way dependent upon such a factor, is entirely mistaken. He insists that the physicist, for example, can only become a physicist, and can only acquire the skill and determination to perform his experiments, if he is integrated into the living community of physicists, apart from which that science, as we know it, could not exist. In other words, the individual physicist, however eminent, can only be what he is in the setting of that community. Even so, he argues, the Christian can only come to be what he is through the influence of the Christian community. He points out that the most significant element in any society of whatever kind is the 'spirit' of the society, which characterizes the society as a whole. *A fortiori*, must this hold good in the case of Christianity, which is rooted in the Spirit-bearing Body, which is the Church.

The implication of all this for Christian morality is sufficiently clear. However 'empirical' Christian moral theology may be, the experiments can be performed adequately only within the life of the community and under the authority of the community. It is just as much a delusion to suppose that the individual Christian can perform satisfactory moral experiments apart from the life of the Christian community as it is to suppose that a person could perform the difficult and exacting experiments demanded by physics independently. In other words, empiricism is well enough;

but to perform experiments that are going to give fruitful results is not such a simple matter as is sometimes supposed. Granted that Christian moral theology should seek to be empirical so far as may be, we have to be very careful to understand what are the conditions in which the experiments can be fruitfully performed, and what results we are entitled to expect.

We proceed, then, to consider the precise nature and the limitations of the empirical approach to Christian moral theology. In the first place, we note that, as a general rule, experiment can be rightly and properly made only within the setting of community.[1] Thus we have seen that the physicist can carry out his difficult and exacting experiments only in the community life of physicists. Not only do they co-operate in the performance of any elaborate experiment, but they support one another by a common faith and determination. Moreover, the skills which they have acquired as members of a team have been acquired in community. We might, therefore, expect that, *mutatis mutandis*, any moral experiments which Christians may make, if they are to succeed, must also be within the Christian community. The individual Christian cannot rightly experiment on his own, without considering the other members of the Church. However difficult this may be, he also has to pay some attention to 'the weaker brother' as St. Paul calls him. So far as possible, he has to avoid putting a stumbling block in the way of another. Moreover, in the case of the Christian community, there is a special reason why the individual Christian must pay attention to the rest of the Body, and that is that it is inspired and guided by the Holy Spirit, whose mind it has or at any rate seeks. Thus St. Paul, in giving moral guidance to the Christians at Ephesus, warns them not to 'grieve the Holy Spirit of God' (*Eph.* 4. 30). In writing to the Romans he says to them:

[1] Of course, there are exceptions to the rule.

'Your conduct is no longer guided by love' (*N.E.B.* translation of *Rom.* 14. 15) if they fail to remember the other members of the Body. Thus we see that 'love' (*agape*) is regarded as the indispensable criterion by which Christian conduct must be judged, and 'love' in the New Testament is a community word.

A good deal has been written and said about the meaning of *agape.* Perhaps the word is untranslatable; but one thing at least is clear about its meaning—and this is relevant to what we are saying—and that is that it is a community word. Basically it reflects the life of the Blessed Trinity, who is 'love,' which was manifested in the Incarnation of the Son of God, and which is poured into the hearts (*sc.* minds) of the faithful through the Holy Spirit (*Rom.* 5. 5). To be possessed of *agape* will indeed not always make it clear what course of action is right,[1] but at least it can be said that without it any action will be less than fully Christian. As the course of human history moves on, new problems of conduct and new difficulties complicating old problems are bound to emerge. The challenge is in the first instance to the Christian community. The way may not be—indeed, usually is not—immediately clear. What is clear is that, unless Christians possess *agape* among themselves, they cannot expect to be able to see what *agape* will mean towards the world and in the world.

At this point we must turn aside to consider briefly the position taken by some modern writers, of whom Bishop Robinson in his brilliantly publicized but too hastily written book, *Honest to God*, is typical. In this book it is maintained that love is the sole ethical criterion; not only in the sense that 'nothing else makes a thing right or wrong,'[2] but also in the sense that all that matters ethically is 'the deepest welfare of these particular persons in this particular situation.'[3] It is thus assumed that we can isolate moral problems

[1] See p. 51.   [2] *Op. cit.*, p. 119.   [3] *Ibid.*, p. 118.

as they confront a given individual, or given individuals, from their wider social reference. If we understand 'love,' as St. John understands it, as a kind of shorthand description of the nature and being of God, we need not quarrel with the contention that 'love' is what makes an action right. But it certainly does not follow from this that love is concerned only with 'the deepest welfare of these particular persons.' This is a proposition which is by no means self-evident, and which must be supported by reasoned argument; but none is forthcoming. In point of fact, those who sponsor this position do not adhere to it consistently. Thus in the debate on the permissibility of contraceptives in marriage, they are insistent that it is *not* only the husband and the wife whose interests are to be consulted, but the welfare of the family as a whole. There is force in this argument, but, if it is accepted, it completely overthrows Bishop Robinson's position. Moreover, it is in accordance with a truly empirical approach, which must not seek to restrict the field in which experiment takes place. We shall have to return to this whole question in the next chapter. Here it is enough to say that the position adopted by Bishop Robinson is as arbitrary and *a priori* as that of the most rigid legalist.

After this brief digression, we can now pass on to consider what results may be expected from the experimental method in moral theology, if the experiments are carried out in the general manner which has been indicated.

We observe, then, in the first place, that to make a scientific experiment is to put a question to Nature in such wise that she is compelled to give an answer. But it is always a question concerning fact. Is the wave theory of light true or is the corpuscular theory true? Is magnetism identical with electricity or is it not? and so forth. All experiments in science are based on an attempt to discover how far our theories correspond to facts. It follows, therefore, that to adopt the empirical approach to an ethical question is to put to Nature a question of fact. That is the most that can be expected from this approach. But morals is never entirely a question of fact, because ethics is a normative science. It is concerned not only with facts but also with values, good or bad, right or wrong. Scientific procedure can never provide an answer to a question of values. It is true that 'by their fruits ye shall know them' and the empirical approach enables us to discover with varying degrees of accuracy what *are* the fruits of a particular line of conduct; but it cannot tell us whether the fruits are good or bad. In order to discover that we are driven back to first principles of law and right.

We may illustrate this by considering further the problem of artificial contraception. The traditional approach was to regard it from the standpoint of natural law. The now familiar argument ran that the primary purpose of coitus is generation; therefore every act of coitus must be *aptus ad generationem* in the sense that it is illegitimate to introduce into the act any factor which would deliberately make generation impossible. For this would make the act contrary to nature, being designed to prevent the primary purpose of coitus. Moreover, it is argued, allowing for the existence of secondary purposes of coition in drawing together the spouses in the marital relationship, the use of contraceptive devices cannot leave even that aspect of coitus unaffected since the parties are fully aware that they are artificially interfering with a natural act by seeking to obstruct it, and conscientious scruples—even if they are unconscious—are likely to be aroused. If they are unconscious, they are not less damaging; the reverse is the case.

The empirical approach to this problem, on the other hand, is to regard the use of contraceptives as an experiment designed to ask Nature the question whether their use does in point of fact damage the marriage relationship. Does the evidence show that such scruples are in general to be found? Is it a fact that the use of contraceptives does diminish self-control? Moreover, it is argued that in this context Nature must be understood in a wide sense to include not only the man and his wife but also the children.[1] Nature must be asked, therefore, whether families in which contraceptives are used are, so far as can be judged, more balanced and happy than those in which they are not? It is clear that in order to be able to discover with any degree of certainty what answer Nature gives to these questions is not at all easy. In debates on this subject, which are sometimes conducted with more heat than light, it is common to hear confident answers given affirmatively to these questions, but the evidence is seldom, if ever, scientifically set out—for the simple reason that it is extraordinarily difficult to obtain.

Let us take another example, that of divorce. The empirical approach to this question is to consider the evidence on both sides. On the one side, it is clear that there are numerous cases in which a second union has proved to be a very happy one, whereas the first had been a miserable failure—and that on both sides. There is also the evidence of the harmful effect on the children of living in a home in which the parents are openly quarrelling and at variance. It is also said on this side that the evidence in some cases is that the marriage has been entered upon so lightly and ill-advisedly that it is almost blasphemous to suggest that the couple has been joined together by God. But it is not always borne in mind that the Prayer Book formula 'Those whom God has joined together let no man put asunder' is entirely different from the Scriptural formula which is: '*What* God hath joined together let not man put asunder' (*Mark* 10. 9).

---

[1] It is significant that the exclusive appeal to the individual or the individual couple is here abandoned, as has already been pointed out.

On the other side there is also empirical evidence. In the first place, stands the evidence of the harm which is done to the institution of marriage by the practice of divorce. A divorce may ease the path for the individuals concerned, but every divorce is a blow against the institution of marriage. The multiplication of divorces leads inevitably to the multiplication of hasty and ill-assorted marriages; for, obviously, the easier divorce appears to be the more light-heartedly will men and women tend to enter into marriage. Thus a vicious circle is set up, and the evidence clearly points to this. In the second place, if the door of divorce is standing open all the time, it puts an additional strain on a young couple which may undermine their confidence and resolution in surmounting the 'teething troubles' which beset many marriages at first. The temptation to walk out may be too great and lead to disaster. Thirdly, with regard to the children, it is universally agreed that the evidence clearly shows that a broken home invariably has harmful effects upon the children. Indeed, it might appear to show that even a home in which the parents are at loggerheads is better from the point of view of the children than one which breaks up altogether.

Now where does all this evidence lead? Who can essay with confidence to assess it? In other words, if we regard divorce as an experiment in which we are putting a question to Nature, what is the answer that she gives? Does she say Yes or No to divorce?

The upshot of what has been said would seem to be somewhat as follows. The empirical approach to questions of morals, though legitimate and desirable in all questions where there is moral doubt, in practice is apt to lead to inconclusive results. In other words, moral experiments are apt to break down, because it is so often extremely difficult to assess the evidence. Furthermore, it has to be recognized that even when the experiment leads to clear findings, these

D

findings can never be more than factual. In the end we are
forced back in all questions of morals to the realm of law
and first principles. Every system of morality which does
not seek to explain it away must come to rest finally on basic
conceptions of right or good which cannot be demonstrated,
but must be accepted—call it natural law or what you will.
Morality cannot dispense with first principles of this kind
without ceasing to be morality.

It is rather difficult to understand why anybody, at least
anybody who accepts the authority of the New Testament,
should boggle at this. Since, however, there are, in fact,
many who think that the whole conception of law is alien
to the Christian ethic, we must pass on to consider the
objections which are raised.

The first objection which we may consider is the objection
to the idea of rules as being inconsistent with the whole
conception of Christian morality. It is, I think, sometimes
forgotten by those who adopt this standpoint that *regula*
and *exemplum* in Latin both mean the same thing, a model
or a pattern; and those who object to rules in connexion
with morality do not hesitate to accept the idea of morality
as following a good example, especially the example of our
Lord. *Imitatio Christi*, indeed, is universally admitted to be
very near the heart of the Christian ethic. But as soon as
the word 'rule' or 'rules' is mentioned, opposition is apt to
be aroused. Thus a recent writer on moral theology says:
'There is an inherent contradiction in trying to achieve
holiness by means of a system of rules. It is not a question
of the adequacy or inadequacy of any particular set of rules;
it is the whole conception of holiness as the same kind of
thing as legality which is unsatisfactory. Almost everyone
agrees that Acts of Parliament cannot make people good;
but it is not so often recognized, although I hope to show
that it is just the same principle, that rules of life cannot
make people saints. The man who sets out to be a saint by

keeping to a rule of life is not the typical Christian but the typical Pharisee. He has a noble aim and may be deeply sincere, but he is on the wrong lines.'[1] Of course, it is true that obedience to laws can be abused and lead either to spiritual pride, on the one hand, or to spiritual despair on the other. That is not to the point. The point is whether laws and rules *per se* are inconsistent with the Christian ethic. My submission is that they are not, but that, on the contrary, they are essential to it. But they must be properly understood and properly approached.

For the understanding of the true meaning of law, as a Christian should see it, we cannot do better than turn to the famous account of it given by the judicious Hooker in Book I of his *Ecclesiastical Polity*. 'A law therefore generally taken, is a directive rule unto goodness of operation. The rule of divine operations outward is the definitive appointment of God's own wisdom set down within himself.'[2] And he concludes this Book with the words: 'Of law there can be no less acknowledged than that her seat is the bosom of God, her voice the harmony of the world: all things in heaven and earth do her homage, the very least as feeling her care, and the greatest as not exempted from her power: both Angels and men and creatures of what condition soever, though each in different sort and manner, yet all with uniform consent, admiring her as the mother of their peace and joy.'[3] Moral law, therefore, means nothing less than a glimpse into the mind of God. Thus the law against stealing and lying is wrong because these actions are not in accordance with the mind of God. God is true and no deceiver. A deceitful God is not God whom we as men could worship and adore. All moral laws, accordingly, are disclosures to man of the mind of God.

Of course, we must avoid the dangerous error of supposing that this means that we have full knowledge of the mind of

[1] H. Oppenheimer: *Law and Love* (1962), p. 19.   [2] *Op. cit.* I. § 4.   [3] *Ibid.*

God. Hooker warns us against this error. 'That law, which hath been the pattern to make, and is the card to guide the world by; that law which hath been of God and with God everlastingly; that law, the author and observer whereof is only one God to be blessed for ever; how should either men or angels be able perfectly to behold? The book of this law we are neither able nor worthy to open and look into. That little whereof we darkly apprehend we admire, the rest with religious ignorance we humbly and meekly adore.'[1]

It must be pointed out in this connexion that there is no inconsistency at all between regarding morality and moral principles as proceeding from the will of God and at the same time as being the law of man's nature and self-fulfilment, unless, of course, they are regarded as the *arbitrary* dictates of God. Professor D. M. Mackinnon surprisingly makes this assumption, when he criticizes the traditional Christian approach to morality. He says: 'You cannot have it both ways; either this way of living is commended because it is self-justifying or it is commanded because it is the will of God.'[2] The answer to this objection is simply that we *can* have it both ways, provided that the will of God is not regarded as the volition of a capricious tyrant and that the being of man is seen to proceed from and to reflect the character of the self-same God. This conception, after all, lies at the heart of the traditional conception of the Natural Law as the participation of the human reason—which is the core of what we mean by human nature—in the mind of God. Unfortunately this idea, like the whole conception of natural theology,[3] has been sadly neglected by too many modern theologians.

This leads to a second objection. It is admitted that neither Christian morality, nor any other kind of morality,

---

[1] *Ibid.* § 5.
[2] *Objections to Christian Belief* (1963), p. 15, Essay on Moral Objections.
[3] There is a refreshing appeal for the resuscitation of natural theology in Canon J. S. Bezzant's Essay in the same volume.

can dispense with basic moral principles. It is, however, argued that the advocates of a moral theology based on Natural Law are mistaken because the conception is too vague to provide secure foundations. What (it is asked) are these alleged principles of the Natural Law said to be universally recognized by mankind? In the end they turn out to be so few and so vague as to be of little practical value. Indeed, some would urge that they can be reduced to one, viz. that we should do good and not evil; but this means little unless we are told what kinds of actions are good or bad. As for any other alleged dictates of the Natural Law, it is said that there is not one of them which we do not think it right to contravene in certain circumstances. Thus it may be self-evident that we should not throw our lives away or take the life of another, or neglect our children; and yet most people agree that circumstances may arise in which it is right to do all these things. It is, therefore, argued we should reject entirely the traditional basis of Natural Law and build our moral theology on the Sermon on the Mount. Here, it is said, is the only sure foundation.

This criticism, which is sometimes heard to-day, is important, and we must proceed to examine it with care. It may be admitted at the outset that the Sermon on the Mount is clearly intended to be a practical guide for living. The parable at the end in which are the two builders—on the sand and on the rock respectively—makes this quite certain. It might, therefore, seem reasonable to argue that, since moral theology is concerned with the practical application of Christian moral principles, here is the right basis for moral theology. But when we begin to examine the Sermon carefully with a view to discovering its practical import, we come up against the same difficulty as that which confronted us in Natural Law, i.e. vagueness. What exactly do these injunctions mean in practice? It is pretty

generally agreed by scholars that they must be taken symbo-
lically. To treat them literally would not only be to fly in
the face of Jewish idiom but also impossible in practice.

Once, however, the literal interpretation is abandoned,
we have the same problem of uncertainty. It has been said
that the Sermon does not give us *directions* but *direction*.
This is true. It does undoubtedly indicate a general attitude
to life—a generous and not a grasping attitude, not insistent
upon one's rights, not vindictive. But in practice we need
more than this to guide us along the path of practical
living; and, what is more, it is clear that our Lord himself
gave us more direction than this. It is, therefore, surely
difficult to argue that the Sermon gives us fundamentally
all that is needed. This is not to say, indeed, that the Sermon
is not of primary importance as a general approach to moral
theology. It means that any moral theology which is
positively inconsistent with it is to be condemned. But this
is quite a different thing from saying that we should set aside
the traditional basis of Natural Law and substitute for it the
Sermon on the Mount. If there be doubt as to what *are*
the agreed principles of the Natural Law—and the doubt
has certainly been magnified by some writers recently—
there is, to say the least, no less doubt as to the exact interpretation of the Sermon, which has been made to point in
a good many different directions.

The conclusion of this matter seems to be found in two
considerations. On the one hand, the Sermon on the
Mount is undoubtedly inconsistent with a legalistic moral
theology. There is no reasonable doubt about that. On the
other hand, if legalism is, as we have argued, to be carefully
distinguished from law, it is not inconsistent with that. It
is inconsistent with law as we know it at the purely human
level—with what we call legislation—but it is not inconsistent with the belief in basic moral principles which reflect
the mind of God—i.e. with law in the ultimate sense of the

term. The chief trouble with debates on this subject is that opponents of Natural Law doctrine will insist on confusing law with legalism and moral principles with legislation.

This last point leads to the consideration of a third objection. This is usually expressed by saying that our Lord never legislated. This objection is entirely due to the confusion which has just been discussed. Of course our Lord did not legislate in the ordinary sense of the term, as men legislate. But he did lay down the law. As Mr. Trevor Hughes has recently said: 'It is possible to claim that He asked too much; it is not possible to say that He did away with laws, duties and standards.'[1] We know that, at the Last Supper, he explicitly claimed to be instituting a new covenant, and that, in the mind of a Hebrew, meant laying down a new Law or set of laws. There is no escaping that.

Once this is clearly understood, it ceases to be necessary to attempt to show, as has so often been done, that our Lord's plain and obvious teaching about the law of marriage was, in fact, nothing of the kind. The evidence of the earliest Gospel, that of St. Mark, is clear and unambiguous here. The fact that St. Matthew's version, whether veridical or not, differs from it does not alter the fact that he was claiming to lay down the law. Indeed, the fact that St. Matthew cites a different version confirms this; for if the Marcan version had been understood at the time to be no more than the setting forth of a general ideal at which to aim, there would clearly have been no need to introduce the Matthaean exception.

It is quite true, of course, that our Lord as a rule puts forward his moral teaching in a particular symbolical way so as to avoid, as far as possible, the danger of legalism; but that does not mean that he is not setting forth the new Law.

[1] H. Trevor Hughes: *Faith and Life*, An Introduction to Christian Ethics (1962), p. 51.

Legalism is essentially the state of mind which induces satisfaction by enabling a person to say, or at least to think, that he has fulfilled the law. But if the law is set forth in the kind of way in which it appears in the Sermon on the Mount in vivid symbolic fashion, which demands thoughtful as contrasted with mechanical or formal obedience, this danger is minimized. Of course, the danger of legalism can never be entirely eliminated; it is always possible for a person to congratulate himself that on such and such an occasion (for example) he turned the other cheek or went the second mile. Our Lord, however, is emphatic in teaching that even when one has done one's duty—or assumes that one has done it—there is no room for self-satisfaction. We are taught to say: 'We are servants and deserve no credit: we have only done our duty' (*Luke* 17. 10. *N.E.B.*).

The root difficulty about moral conduct is here laid bare. It does not consist in regarding morality as a law or in seeking to obey rules. It is in the thought that we can gain credit for anything that we do. Christ teaches that this is impossible, because (he implies) our duty is what we owe to God; and even if we succeed completely in doing it (and we know that we cannot) it is still what we owe to God. According to non-theistic systems of ethics it *is* possible to gain moral credit: in Christian theistic ethics it is not possible. So our Lord teaches, and it is one of the basic principles of his teaching, which had not been grasped by the disciples of Moses.

We are entitled to say, therefore, that there is no essential objection to thinking of morality in terms of law. There is no objection to a moral theology based on law, with two provisos. The first is that we must recognize that a moral law is a glimpse into the mind of God, and that we do not as individuals know fully the mind of God. So far as it has been revealed, it has been revealed to the Christian Community, which is the Church, which is inspired by the Holy Spirit. So St. Paul can write: 'For who hath known the mind of the Lord, that he may instruct him? But we have the mind of Christ' (1 *Cor.* 2). The second proviso is that we must clearly understand that we can never fulfil the law, or begin to fulfil the law, except by love (*agape*). And love means that we recognize that we never *can* fulfil the law; for Christian love is a response to the infinite love of God. 'We love, because he first loved us' (1 *John* 4. 19). This love was revealed by our Lord and is conveyed to the faithful in Christ Jesus by the Holy Spirit who is given to them (*Rom.* 5. 5).

Thus moral theology, if it is to be true to the New Testament, must be a moral theology of the Holy Spirit. The Church, which is the living organism of the Spirit, must continually change and grow. 'New occasions teach new duties.' This makes room for the empirical approach, without which law may easily degenerate into legalism. Yet we must not forget that there must always be this difference between the empiricism of natural science and moral empiricism (if that is the right expression). Scientific empiricism leads to a steady growth in scientific knowledge, each generation of scientists, as it were, standing on the shoulders of the previous generation. Christian moral apprehension and growth is more akin to art than to science. Just as art grows when God reveals the eternal beauty to a great artist, so does moral and spiritual apprehension grow when God raises up a prophet in his Church or is pleased to stir some deep movement in the Christian Community.

Thus far we have been defending the legitimacy of the concept of law in moral theology. But we cannot leave the question there. Law is not only necessary in theory because morals must be based on ultimate first principles. It is necessary also in practice. We need moral laws to guide us in our daily life. Take, for example, the law against lying: 'Thou shalt not bear false witness.' This is essential for the average person. Even though there may be exceptional cases where lying is permissible, the law is still required. Exceptions, it is admitted, prove the rule. We must have such moral principles to guide us. It is all very well to say that the Christian should be told to follow the maxim: 'Love and do what you like,' but this is far too vague to meet the practical requirements of moral conduct. This is a question to which we shall have to return later. As Professor Dodd has said: 'Augustine's maxim has the value of a challenging epigram, but it can be seriously misleading.'[1]

There is, however, another reason why rules are required. They set before us a minimum standard below which we must not allow ourselves to fall. It is important to understand this; for the rules of morality are, in this respect, entirely different from civil laws. Civil laws set before us minimum standards which are also maxima. Thus no motorist, however law-abiding, thinks that he should necessarily adopt a 25 m.p.h. speed limit instead of one at 30 m.p.h. Nobody, however conscientious, supposes that if the Inland Revenue requires him to pay 7s. 9d. in the pound for income tax, he ought perhaps to pay 10s. in the pound. It is recognized that these are maxima. But the rules and laws which are set before the Christian are minima but *not* maxima. There are some, indeed, who object to the whole idea of minimum standards for a Christian. They argue that to follow these is less than Christian. We must aim always at perfection. This, however, *strictly interpreted*, means rigorism, which proves to be unworkable, and, moreover, is not what we find in the New Testament. Thus, for example, when the early church met to consider what should be required of Gentile Christians in regard to the observances of the Jewish Law, the strict line would have been to have demanded these; but, as St. Peter said, this would be to lay upon them 'a yoke which neither we

[1] C. H. Dodd: *Gospel and Law* (1951), p. 72.

nor our fathers were able to bear.' The Apostles, therefore, refused to do this. Instead, they laid down a minimum standard for the Gentiles to follow. If we reject this approach, we can be allowed no relaxations at all, and life becomes grim in the extreme. Moreover, if we are scrupulous in tendency it becomes impossible. We are continually tortured by doubts as to whether we *have* followed the highest, insomuch that we have no time to live a normal life at all. In the end our pursuit of perfection has brought us down to a far lower level than if we had pitched our aim a little lower. Experience shows that we cannot do without rules and laws to guide us. In other words, the path to perfection may be to follow humbly along the road of a simple rule which is not too exacting—for most individuals this is certainly true. This is a question to which we shall have to return.

Additional Note on St. Matthew 5. 17

It is becoming fashionable among some modern Christian moralists to assume that the meaning of 'fulfil' (*plerosai*) in this passage is virtually 'to abolish by transcending.' Thus, for example, Canon D. A. Rhymes in his recently published *No New Morality* writes: 'The whole tenor of His (*sc.* Christ's) teaching was not to further the law, or even to substitute another law of His own, but to "fulfil the law"— that is to concern Himself with fulfilment in the life of man rather than with codes and regulations.' There is no evidence at all for such an interpretation of *plerosai* in this passage. Professor A. Guillaume pointed out a long time ago that no Talmudic lexicon contains an etymological equivalent of *pleroun* used in this sense. He argued that the Talmudic equivalent must be the idiomatic phrase 'to make to stand that which is said,' which is almost the exact opposite of this modern interpretation. (See *The Expository Times*, vol. 37, No. 9, p. 394.) This understanding of the passage is endorsed by Dr. David Daube (*The New Testament and Rabbinical Judaism*, Univ. of London Press, 1956, pp. 60 f.).

CHAPTER 4

THE CHRISTIAN MORAL STANDARD

SOMETHING has already been said about the ethical standard or standards which confront the Christian; but the matter demands closer examination, because the whole conception of an absolute moral standard is challenged by some who claim to be Christians. They maintain, as we have seen, that 'love' rather than standards or laws is the only ethical criterion. This position is all the more surprising in that, so far as we know, our Lord never said anything even remotely like this in his teaching. Thus, for example, when the rich young ruler[1] came to him and inquired what he should do in order to 'inherit eternal life,' he told him to keep the commandments and proceeded to enumerate some of them. When the young man replied that he was already doing this, our Lord, even then, did not say, 'But you still need "love,"' or words to that effect. He told him to observe the rules of poverty—surrender all his possessions —obedience—follow him—and this meant also (for the time being at least) celibacy. What an opportunity our Lord missed of driving home his own teaching! It would have been so simple to say: 'Love and do what you like.'

Once again, in the so-called Sermon on the Mount, there is no saying of this nature. On the contrary, our Lord here gives definite instructions as to how to behave in specifically mentioned circumstances. The fact that these injunctions are delivered in highly symbolical terms does not alter this. We are told how we should, as his disciples, behave when tempted to anger, or to lust, or to perjury, or to retaliation, or to meanness, or by the false claims of nationalism. We

[1] Mark 10. 17 ff.

are told how to observe the recognized duties of almsgiving, prayer and fasting. How should this be, if the Christian ethic is summed up in the command: Love and do what you like?

As is well known, this dictum comes from St. Augustine; but those who quote it seldom, if ever, cite the context in which it occurs. Since these new apostles of the ethic of 'love' appeal to St. Augustine, to Augustine they shall go.

The Augustinian dictum in question exists in two forms, and in two contexts. It will therefore be convenient to begin by considering both versions in their respective contexts. The first of these, and that most commonly quoted is: *Dilige et quod vis fac.* In this passage Augustine is considering how the love of God was manifested to man. It was (he quotes Romans 8. 32) when God spared not his own Son but gave him up (*tradidit*) for us all. But, he says, Judas Iscariot also gave him up (*tradidit*). Indeed, our Lord gave himself up (*tradidit*) for me, says St. Paul. How, then, does the 'giving up' differ in these three cases? Augustine answers: 'Because the Father and the Son did this through love (*in caritate*), but Judas did it as a traitor. You see, then, that it is not what a man does which has to be considered, but with what motive and will he does it.'[1] If the root—i.e. the motive of the action—is love, the action cannot but be good. Therefore, says Augustine, love and do what you will.

The argument is not a good one, and it lends little support to the present-day advocates of an all-love ethic. It is quite true that if love, in the sense of caring for others, is the motive of our actions we shall not willingly harm them; but that is quite a different thing from saying that we shall always act rightly towards them. Much wrong can be done, and is done every day, by people with good motives —people who 'mean well' as we say, like the kind-hearted

[1] In Ep. Johann. C. 4. Tractatus VII.

elephant which sat on the eggs of the ostrich to keep them warm, when the mother had temporarily left them. More than a kind heart is required for right conduct. It is, indeed, true that previously Augustine had emphasized the saying of the Apostle that God is love (*dilectio*) and this might well have led to a more objective treatment of right-conduct as consisting in a good deal more than conduct proceeding from the right motive; in fact, however, Augustine does not follow this out, and we are left with the highly unsatisfactory argument which we have just considered.

The second version of the Augustinian epigram is: *Dilige ergo, et quidquid volueris fac*. But the context is different: Augustine is here speaking about the command to love our neighbours as ourselves. He says: 'If you love (*diligis*) the whole human race as yourself there remains no door by which sin can find an entrance into you. You close every approach by which the devil enters the soul, if you love all as yourself. Indeed, brethren, how is it possible that anyone can do evil to another person, if he loves him as himself. Love therefore, and do whatever you will' (*Sermo* cvii). This is a rather different version of the same argument and a less vulnerable one; for it does not make love reside solely in the motive. In our relation to ourselves we not only have the motive to do the best for ourselves but we also have a large measure of insight as to what is for our own good. A large measure but not a full measure. We can, and often do, harm ourselves; indeed, many a person is, as the phrase goes, his own worst enemy. This shows clearly that to say 'love God and your neighbours as yourself' does not provide an all-sufficient guide for conduct. Nor did Augustine ever suggest that it does. It is, therefore, quite unfair to quote this epigram, as so often is done, as if he had set it forth as a compendium of Christian morals. In the next sermon Augustine goes on very properly to quote our Lord's words and to say: 'The true love (*dilectio*) consists in the complete keeping of his commands; as he says in another place, "If anyone loves me, let him keep my words." Wherefore the Truth himself says in another place, "Hereby all men shall know that you are my disciples, if you bear love to one another." Again the Apostle says, "Love is the fulfilling of the law." ' It is, therefore, a complete misrepresentation of Augustine to quote him in support of our modern apostles of love, who argue that this is the only Christian moral command or criterion required. In practice, they are far from consistent in the position which they adopt. In one breath, they seem to throw all laws and rules overboard; in the next, they talk about moral rules and conventions as being in practice necessary. To quote one of them, they are 'the dykes of love.'[1]

Later on we shall have to consider more fully why 'love' cannot be held to be adequate as the sole criterion of Christian behaviour. But before we inquire into this, we must ask why it is that there is such a strong revulsion on the part of many against the idea of moral laws, and a desire to substitute 'love' as the sole moral criterion. There seem, in the main, to be two reasons. The first is that it is sometimes clearly right to break a precept of the moral law. Thus our Lord taught that it was right for David to perform what was in fact an act of sacrilege by eating the shewbread in order to obtain food for those who were famished. Moreover, this was also an infringement of the eighth commandment; it was an act of stealing as well. Consequently, it is argued, moral laws can provide no adequate moral criterion. The conclusion does not follow. What emerges from an incident like this is that two or more moral laws may conflict in a particular set of circumstances. In this case three laws were involved: the law of reverence to God, the law that stealing is wrong, and the law requiring us to take food essential for our bodily needs. In such cases, one law can over-ride

---

[1] Robinson: *Honest to God* (1963), p. 118.

another and must do so. But this does not prove that moral laws provide no guidance. In nine cases out of ten, perhaps in ninety-nine cases out of a hundred, sacrilege is wrong and stealing is wrong. The exceptional case—and this was clearly an exceptional case—does not affect this at all. On the contrary, 'the exception proves the rule.' It certainly does not show that we can dispense altogether with moral laws and rules.

The second reason is that whereas it is admittedly some-times right to break moral laws and commandments, it is never right to infringe 'love.' This contention, however, is plausible simply because the conception of love is inevitably so vague that it is always possible to argue that this or that particular action which one wishes to defend was, or is, an act of love. For example, suppose that it is asked whether or not our Lord's action in cleansing the Temple was an act of 'love.' Those who wish to defend it on these grounds can do so, if they wish, and it is impossible to show that they are wrong. On the other hand, it would be equally possible to argue that it was nothing of the kind, but a completely unjustifiable display of temper. It is thus possible to main-tain the thesis that it is never right to infringe 'love' which-ever way we pass judgement on this action. Those who approve the action will say that it was not an infringement of 'love.' Those who disapprove it are equally free to say that it was. Consequently, 'love' as a criterion of right conduct is ultimately too vague to be an adequate moral guide. It may turn out to be equivalent merely to 'moral conduct which I approve.'

This, indeed, is virtually admitted by some of the modern apostles of love. They maintain that 'love' will always find the right way in every set of circumstances. They lay great stress on the particularity of moral judgements. All moral judgements (they claim) must be passed in the light of the needs of 'these particular persons in this particular situation.'[1] There are, therefore, no absolute moral laws or rules—of chastity, for example. In particular circumstances fornication may be the best course of action—indeed, the most Christian course of action. It may, in fact, be the manifestation of Christian love.

It has already been noted that this position which particularizes all moral judgements is assumed, rather than argued. Nevertheless, it is far from self-evident why 'these particular persons' should always be the decisive factor in making a moral judgement. It might seem to be more reasonable to claim that what matters most is the moral well-being of the generality of persons. For example, just because it appears that in a particular case fornication may seem to bring spiritual benefits to an individual person or an individual couple, does that make it right? Are not the moral benefits to society generally rather the criterion of right conduct?

Mr. H. A. Williams, in a notorious essay, has cited the case of a young man who regained his lost self-confidence by sleeping with a girl who was not his wife, and thus was made whole. 'And when there is healing, there is Christ whatever the Church may say about fornication.'[2] It would, however, be possible to cite an analogous case, which might cause even Mr. Williams to hesitate. Suppose the case of a young man who is emotionally drawn to his very attractive young niece. He is thirty years of age and she is twenty. This young man also is a psychopath, without self-confidence, doubtful of his virility. But in the presence of this girl all is different. He seduces her and he finds complete sexual liberation—or so he thinks. He is made whole. Does that mean that the law against incest does not bind? It would not be impossible to think of even more unseemly cases. There is surely a serious confusion of thought here. Of course, good can come out of evil, and evil of the

---

[1] *Honest to God*, p. 118.   [2] *Soundings*, p. 82.

E

deepest dye—the Crucifixion is enough to prove that—but that does not make evil good. Nor does it prove that in making moral judgements it is only the good, or apparent good, of a particular individual or individuals which has to be taken into account. What has to be shown is that the upholding of general moral standards, or principles, or laws —whichever term we may choose—leads ultimately to the production of less good than the disregarding of them. Or, to put the matter the other way round, that what we may call the 'particularist' approach of the modern apostles of love would not, if widely adopted, lead to a serious debasing of the moral currency. This certainly has never been shown to be the case. Indeed, little attempt seems to have been made to show it to be the case. Yet until this is done, the modern 'love' ethic completely lacks validation, and is fraught with the gravest moral dangers to society.

We must, therefore, examine more closely the whole question of the place of laws and moral principles in Christian morality, and their relation to *agape*, or 'love.' It is a question to which insufficient attention has been given. If the charge can be made against the traditional approach to moral theology, based on law, that it has been too much *a priori*, it can also be said with truth that the advocates of a Christian morality based solely on 'love' are equally *a priori*. No progress is likely to be made along that line. What seems to be required is a more thorough examination of the essential meaning of 'law' and the essential meaning of '*agape*.' This might well lead to a reconciliation between the two.

Let us, therefore, turn to a careful consideration of the doctrine of 'love' as it is found in the Scriptures. We must begin with the Old Testament, for it is here that the conception of 'love' (*ahabha*) originates. We find it first in Deuteronomy, where the Decalogue is reinterpreted in terms of love. We read: 'Hear, O Israel, the Lord, our God, is one

Lord: and thou shalt love the Lord thy God with all thine heart, and with all thy soul, and with all thy might. And these words, which I command thee this day, shall be upon thy heart' (*Deut.* 6. 4–6). What this means is clearly indicated in what follows: 'Ye shall diligently keep the commandments of the Lord your God, and his testimonies, and his statutes which he hath commanded thee. And thou shalt do that which is right and good in the sight of the Lord: that it may be well with thee, and that thou mayest go in and possess the good land which the Lord sware unto thy fathers.' It is quite clear from this that 'love' is not identified with sentiment or emotion. Indeed, there is nothing emotional about it. It consists in plain, straight-forward obedience to the commands of God, and in doing what is 'right and good.' Thus there is no suggestion at all that there is any kind of opposition between love and law. The modern antithesis between the two would sound strange in the ears of the Deuteronomist, as it would also in the ears of the writer of Psalm 119.

In the next chapter the author of Deuteronomy introduces the conception of God's love to Israel. This is said to have been exhibited in his choice of Israel to be his people with whom he made a special covenant. So far God's love to man and man's love to God seem to be generically different: there is nothing common to them both.

This same teaching is repeated in Chapter 10 when loving God is equated with obedience to his laws, and God's love is revealed in his choice of Israel. But a new element is introduced in the injunction to 'love the stranger: for ye were strangers in the land of Egypt' (10. 19). 'Love' here cannot mean 'obedience to God': it must bear the meaning of 'lovingkindness' which as *hesedh* is found in the great prophets, especially Hosea (*Hos.* 2. 14–23; 6. 6; 11. 1–4, 8). In this great prophet the idea of 'love' seems to be identified with 'caring,' but the conception is never clearly defined.

The teaching of Hosea is taken up in the New Testament and developed by our Lord himself. He explicitly quotes the passage from Hosea 6 in defence of his habit of consorting with disreputable people (*Matt.* 9. 10–13). Love (*hesedh*) obviously involves a deep care for humanity. It is the core of the 'compassion' which our Lord experienced in the presence of the unshepherded multitude (*Matt.* 9. 36, cf. *Luke* 10. 33; 15. 12). As a broad motive underlying his whole earthly life it is plainly fundamental. It is St. John, as we should expect, who brings out the significance of this most fully, especially in his brief but pregnant remark: 'We love because he first loved us' (1 *John* 4. 19)—not 'we love him because he first loved us.' That is not the true text, nor is it nearly so illuminating. The point is that we understand the meaning of what our love (both to God and man) ought to be by considering the meaning of God's love to us—revealed in the Incarnation of our Lord. 'In this was manifested the love of God towards us, because that God sent his only begotten Son into the world, that we might live through him' (4. 9). Our Lord had taught verbally that the love of man must imitate the love of God and therefore be absolutely indiscriminate (*Matt.* 5. 43–45). And what he taught by word, he taught in act by the sheer fact of his holy incarnate life.

Thus the core of the Christian doctrine of 'love' (*agape*)— virtually a new word for a new quality of life—is found in the Incarnation, whereby the Son of God 'for us men and for our Salvation came down from heaven . . . and was made man.' In this sublime act of condescension our Lord put himself in our place. Herein, therefore, is the meaning of Christian love. It is imaginatively to put oneself in the other person's place, and to do to him as we would that he should do to us if we stood in his shoes. That is what it means to love our neighbour as ourselves. Likewise to love God is imaginatively to put ourselves in God's place—look at the world and mankind through God's eyes—and act accordingly. We can do even this by reason of the Incarnation, which opens to us the mind of God as fully as man has the capacity to comprehend it. It is significant that when our Lord was teaching us that 'love' involves loving our enemies, he immediately follows this up by adding that it means praying for them; for by praying for a person we learn to put ourselves in his place, and it is only by doing this, on the other hand, that we can really and truly pray for him. Our Lord showed us this upon the Cross when he prayed for his murderers. He was able even in his dying agony to put himself in their place and to realize that they knew not what they were doing. On the Godward side, the whole of his incarnate life was lived in the light of the Father. To see life through his Father's eyes was, as he said, meat and drink to him.

This is often said to be expressed in what is known as the Golden Rule, 'As ye would that men should do to you do ye also to them likewise' (*Luke* 6. 31; cf. *Matt.* 7. 12). This, however, must be carefully interpreted. It says, '*as* ye would' not '*what* ye would.' Still less does it say, 'Do to them what they would like you to do to them'. Both these misinterpretations land us in moral confusion and even absurdity.[1] The Rule means, as we have said, that we should imaginatively put ourselves in the place of others and treat them as we ourselves could reasonably wish to be treated if we were in their place—*at least* that. This is what it is to treat them with *agape*. Clearly it presupposes some standard by which to decide what *is* reasonable, and this throws us back on the natural principle of what is fair and right. As William Temple pointed out, although Christian love transcends justice it also presupposes it.[2]

[1] See the article on 'The Golden Rule,' by M. G. Singer, in *Philosophy* (October, 1963).
[2] See W. Temple: *Citizen and Churchman* (1941), ch. 5.

St. John even ventures to go so far as to say that God is love in order to bring out his meaning; but it must be carefully noted that he does not say 'Love is God,' but rather 'Love is of God' (1 *John* 4. 7). Love (*agape*) is, after all, an abstraction, and God is not an abstraction but, on the contrary, *ens realissimum*. St. John's meaning, therefore, seems to be that love is a revelation of the innermost nature of God—a doctrine which St. Augustine was later to employ in order to elucidate the mystery of the Holy Trinity.

It is at this point that we are enabled to see the connexion between law and love. The tendency to put these into opposition has been most unfortunate. There is no antithesis between them, if we understand Law as Hooker, for example, understood it as the revelation of the mind of God; for this is exactly how St. John understands love. The error has arisen because we have too frequently interpreted law in the light of man's imperfect 'laws.' This is as serious a mistake as the attribution to personality in God of the limitations of human personality as we know it.

Human law, we have seen, consists in the establishing of minimum standards, which are also maxima. Divine law, on the other hand, is the setting forth of God's perfect standards. Our Lord taught us to remember this always and never to allow ourselves to think that we have completely fulfilled God's law. To the last we remain 'unprofitable servants' (*Luke* 17. 10). At the same time it is true, as we have already seen, that if we are to make spiritual progress at all we need definite rules and laws to guide us. The path to perfection necessarily involves these, for human nature—that is, fallen human nature—is a frail thing.

Thus the Christian moral standard is involved in a paradox. On the one hand, the standard we seek is nothing less than the perfection for which God has made us. We can never 'count ourselves to have apprehended.' On the other hand, in practice we are most likely to achieve it by not aiming directly at it, and following a humbler path.

Once we bring law and love together, we can understand this. Love knows no end. As Aristotle would say, it goes to infinity. When we love another truly we never reach a point at which we can sit back and say: 'I have loved him enough; it is time to stop.' Love endures to the end, as St. Paul says.

On the other hand, we cannot all at once achieve perfect love—either towards God or our neighbour. It has been the mistake of the perfectionist to forget this. We must advance gradually towards perfection, and we can do this only by means of limited objectives in the form of simple rules which are within our reach. So long as we are continually advancing and do not forget that these rules are minima which we hope to outgrow, we are saved from the danger which attaches to the keeping of rules.

This, as Bishop Kirk pointed out, is the valid version of the doctrine of the double-standard in Christian morality. It is not that some are called to perfection and some are not; for all are so called. It is that we do not and cannot become perfect all at once. He rightly says: 'The rigorist conception of the Christian becoming perfect in a moment is an idle and dangerous fiction. We must not daunt the immature Christian by laying on him too heavy a burden at once. He must take his life by stages, achieving what is possible here and now, and not attempting to higher flights until he has exercised himself in the lower ones.'[1] This, as he points out, is the real meaning of the distinction between 'precepts' and 'counsels of perfection'[2] (1 *Cor.* 7. 6). Moreover, we have to pursue the ideal of perfection through particular circumstances—and not in the abstract—and this is an additional reason why we usually need the guidance of specific rules and duties. Provided that we do not follow

[1] K. E. Kirk: *The Vision of God* (1925), p. 243.   [2] *Ibid.*

them slavishly and are never content to think that we have done all that is required of us, they are not harmful, but beneficial and, indeed, necessary.

In the first instance, moral laws and rules represent the authority of inherited experience. Take the Ten Commandments, for example. There is no reason to doubt that they were transmitted to the Hebrews through the medium of a great religious genius, Moses. But we need not suppose that Moses thought them all up out of his own head, or that God gave them to him 'out of the blue.' We know, for example, that Hammurabi had already put forward a similar code. Experience had evidently shown that this kind of conduct was necessary for the stability of society. Respect for the authority of parents, truth-telling, regard for the property of others, monogamous marriage, respect for human life: these things are the cement of human society. Experience clearly indicates that these are rules of behaviour which must be reverenced. They must, therefore, be taught to the young.

After all, we all begin our lives under the authority of various human traditions. That is why we are sent to school. We do not have to begin the study of science, for example, from scratch. We take over a body of scientific knowledge and make it the basis for our further studies. So with historical knowledge, knowledge of music, and of art. The same holds good of moral knowledge, i.e. knowledge of how to behave. We do not each of us have to think this out for ourselves. It would be as absurd to attempt this as to work out our own system of chemistry or physics.

As time goes on, we may, of course, be led to question the truth of this inherited knowledge; but this does not alter the fact that it is quite indispensable and, furthermore, that we have to be very sure of our ground before we jettison long-established tradition.

All this clearly goes to show that we really need the help of tradition in morals, as in everything else, and this tradition is embodied in moral laws and rules. It would be useless simply to tell a young child that he must love other people as himself and do as he would be done by, and leave it at that. We have to be more specific and teach him to speak the truth and keep his hands from picking and stealing, and so forth. Nor is it by any means only children who need the help of such moral laws. If we are honest with ourselves we recognize that we all need them. Life is not long enough to think out afresh the propriety of every action which we perform. We may indeed come to see that in particular circumstances the law which (for example) forbids lying may have to be set aside. This, however, does not alter the fact that to follow the rule of speaking the truth is for 99 per cent of our life the right rule to follow.

Moral laws and rules, then, convey to us the riches of inherited moral experience, and they are the great time-savers. Without them we should be so fully occupied in thinking out our daily conduct that we should have little time for anything else. We should, in fact, all be in the position of the scrupulous person who is so busy trying to decide what to do that he has no time to do anything. Life becomes a perpetual dither. To tell a scrupulous person to love God and his neighbour and that is all that is required of him would be to torture and torment his soul. Although fortunately the majority of persons are not afflicted with scrupulous consciences, there would certainly be many more if the only moral advice which was available was: Love and do what you like. Moreover, those who were not rendered scrupulous would in many cases be victimized by the dangerous tendency to be sentimental about morals. As Professor Dodd has said of this modern love-ethic: 'It is too much exposed to the danger of a barren sentimentality, which is far removed from the temper of the New Testament. The teachers of the early church certainly were not content to leave it at that. The First Epistle of John brings it down to earth in this author's crude and pedestrian way. He writes: "If anyone possesses the means of earthly existence and sees his brother in want, and shuts his heart against him, how can the divine charity dwell in him?" (1 *John* 3. 17).'[1] Mr. Trevor Hughes has rightly said: 'The neglect of laws, duties and standards in the Christian life leads to moral and spiritual flabbiness. The Christian way is a pilgrimage not a hitch-hike. It demands the discipline associated with an expedition, rather than the leisurely attitude of the traveller with a "go as you please" holiday ticket.'[2]

This brings us to the consideration of an important question. What is the connexion between Christian 'love' (*agape*) and 'liking'? It has sometimes been supposed that the command to love is a command to like. This, however, is a serious misunderstanding. Indeed, if it were true, it would completely stultify the Christian ethic; for it is impossible to 'like' anybody to order. Liking is an emotional attraction towards another person and it is a commonplace to say that we cannot by our own volition directly control our emotions. If sufficient attention had been paid to the fact that the command to love our neighbour is to love him 'as thyself,' this misunderstanding would never have arisen; for loving ourselves certainly does not mean the same as liking ourselves. In fact, we do not by any means always like ourselves, nor is it right that we should. Frequently we hate ourselves for the things we have said and done and would give anything to unsay and undo them. On the other hand, we love ourselves all the time—in the sense that we care about ourselves and are interested in ourselves. This gives us the clue to what it means to love our neighbour, and indeed to love God. It is to care for our neighbour and

[1] *Gospel and Law*, p. 72.   [2] H. Trevor Hughes: *Faith and Life* (1962), p. 53.

to be interested in him. This in practice means acting towards him *as if* we felt like this, in the first instance. The end result will be that we shall come to be more and more interested in him. Yet even then we shall not necessarily 'like' him, as we like our personal friends. Likewise, loving God means 'caring for the things of the Lord' (1 *Cor.* 7. 32). It means, *in the first instance*, not an emotional attraction towards God, but merely a desire to further his interests— specified in the Lord's Prayer as hallowing his name, seeking the coming of his kingdom, doing his will.

There are, however, important differences here between loving God and loving our neighbour. We have said that to love our neighbour need not imply liking our neighbour; for in fact our neighbour is not by any means always likeable. But God is pure Goodness, and as we get more and more to know him, loving him means liking him, and enjoying his presence even as we enjoy the presence of our friends.

Furthermore, as Christians we not only learn to love God in the sense of liking him, but there is supplied to us an additional motive for loving our neighbour. We learn to love, and ultimately perhaps even to like, our neighbour because we recognize that he is dear to our Lord. He is 'the brother for whom Christ died' (1 *Cor.* 8. 11). We learn to see more in our neighbour even than that; for our Lord taught us not only that he is identified with his Body the Church, but also that he is identified with every man. Even as early as the date of St. Paul's conversion, it was clearly understood that Christ is identified with the Church. To persecute the Church is to persecute our Lord: 'Saul, Saul, why persecutest thou *me*?' (*Acts* 9. 4). Indeed, our Lord taught in the parable of the last Judgement that he is in some sense to be identified with every man. 'Inasmuch as ye have done it unto one of the least of these my brethren, ye have done it unto me' (*Matt.* 25. 40). All this means that it is (however difficult) easier for a Christian to love, and even to like, his fellow men than for anybody else. He is supplied with a new and powerful motive. Yet it is still important to distinguish between 'loving' and 'liking.' Loving means 'caring,' even as a human parent naturally cares for his child. But this certainly does not mean liking him, if he is a wicked and reprobate character. In the same way we all naturally 'care for' ourselves, even when we hate and loathe ourselves and our past conduct.

CHAPTER 5

CONSCIENCE AND HUMAN RESPONSIBILITY

EVERY book on moral theology has a good deal to say about Conscience. It is a conception which stands at the heart of the subject; and it is one which has been very severely treated in modern times. If the Christian moralist to-day is to gain a hearing, he has to substantiate the claims of conscience and interpret it in such a way as to meet the various modern attempts to 'debunk' it. I say 'it,' but we must beware of the dangerous tendency to reify psychological states of mind, as if they were things. Words like conscience, emotion, feeling or idea can be most misleading if they cause us to forget that we are not dealing with entities but states of mind.

Broadly speaking, there have been, and still are, three different ways of understanding conscience. The first is to regard it as essentially a cognitive function. Thus, for example, Aquinas speaks of it as 'the mind passing moral judgements';[1] and Jeremy Taylor says it is 'the mind of a man governed by a rule.'[2] The second way of understanding it has been to think of it as being a distinctive mode of perception—what has been called 'a moral sense' comparable to, though significantly different from, the five senses. Thus it is concerned with individual situations, and is, in general, to be relied upon, even if it is not infallible. The third way of regarding conscience is to think of it as merely a subjective feeling of approval or disapproval. According to this view, it has no objective significance at all.

We must begin by considering the last of these three approaches, for, if it is valid, it must lead to the complete

[1] S.T. I. Q. 79 a. 13.   [2] *Ductor Dubitantium*, I, 1.

destruction of moral theology by rendering the authority of conscience nugatory. The parent of all modern theories of morality of this kind was David Hume; we must, therefore, begin with him. Hume taught a doctrine which 'maintains that morality is determined by sentiment. It defines virtue to be whatever mental action or quality gives to a spectator the pleasing sentiment of approbation; and vice the contrary.'[1] A careful examination of human experience, Hume argues, makes it clear that the objects of our experience which elicit that response are such as are either useful or agreeable to ourselves or to others. 'Celibacy, fasting, penance, mortification, self-denial, humility, silence, solitude, and the whole train of monkish virtues; for what reason are they everywhere rejected by men of sense, but because they serve to no manner of purpose; neither advance a man's fortune in the world, nor render him a more valuable member of society; neither qualify him for the entertainment of company, nor increase his power of self-enjoyment? We observe, on the contrary, that they cross all these desirable ends; stupefy the understanding and harden the heart, obscure the fancy and sour the temper. We justly, therefore, transfer them to the opposite column, and place them in the catalogue of vices.'[2]

In our own day this emotive theory of morals has found expression in the philosophy of logical positivism and linguistic analysis, although it has moved much further along the path of Hume. Hume, despite his subjectivism, could write: 'The end of all moral speculations is to teach us our duty'[3] although he has, in fact, little to say about duty, and no explanation of moral obligation.[4] But for the modern disciples of Hume ethics has no such object. The task of the

---

[1] *An Enquiry Concerning the Principles of Morals*, Appendix I.
[2] *Ibid.*, IX. 1.   [3] *Ibid.*, I.
[4] 'When the neglect or non-performance of an action displeases us after a like manner, we say that we lie under an obligation to perform it.' *A Treatise of Human Nature*, III, Sect. 5. This is Hume at his weakest.

moral philosopher is purely descriptive and confined to an analysis of the meaning of ethical language. Thus, for example, Professor Ayer says: 'We reject the subjectivist view that to call an action right, or a thing good, is to say that it is generally approved of, because it is not self-contradictory to assert that some actions which are generally approved of are not right, or that things which are generally approved of are not good. And we reject the alternative subjectivist view that a man who asserts that a certain action is right, or that a certain thing is good, is saying that he himself approves of it, on the ground that a man who confessed that he sometimes approved of what was bad or wrong would not be contradicting himself.'[1] Thus, according to Ayer, ethical statements are not factual and verifiable, but purely emotive. To say that an act is wrong is merely to express an emotion; it is not even to make a statement that I experience this emotion. Consequently it is impossible to find a criterion for determining the validity of ethical judgements—and the same is true of aesthetic judgements—because they have no validity. If a sentence makes no statement, it is nonsensical to ask whether it is true or false. How, then, it must be asked, is it that men can dispute about moral questions? To this Ayer, and those who share his standpoint, would say that one never does dispute about questions of moral value, but only about matters of fact.[2] Thus we could argue with somebody as to whether the Inquisition was or was not cruel; but if he claimed that cruelty was a good thing and we held the contrary opinion there would be no point in argument. Argument on moral questions, in other words (it is claimed), is possible only if some system of values is presupposed. Consequently ethical philosophy consists simply in saying that ethical concepts

[1] A. J. Ayer: *Language, Truth and Logic* (2nd edn., 1962 impression), p. 104.
[2] O. A. Johnson has shown that this factually is not true. See his article *On Moral Disagreements*, Mind, (N.S.) Vol. 68, pp. 482.

are pseudo-concepts and therefore unanalysable. The further task of analysing ethical feelings is the task of the psychologist. The only information which can be gathered from the study of aesthetic and moral experiences, therefore, is information about our mental and physical make-up.

The basic objection to this approach to the problem of morals is that it does not square with our experience. In other words, it is not truly empirical. It is an attempt to force moral experience into the mould of a pre-conceived logical theory. Thus an impartial examination of experience makes it quite clear that moral 'feelings' are based upon moral judgements, and not vice versa. The reason why I am indignant when I see a child or an animal being brutally treated is because I judge cruelty to be wrong. In those circumstances when I experience indignation, but further reflection makes it clear to me that this 'moral feeling' is derived from some personal interest, I recognize that my judgement was not a moral judgement at all, but a rationalization, like that of Judas Iscariot when he complained at the waste of money on the costly ointment. Thus, when I say 'Stealing is wrong' I am not, as Ayer suggests, simply expressing my personal disapproval of it. I am suggesting that everybody *ought* to disapprove it, even if they do not; for that is the truth. This is implicit in every moral judgement. It claims to be a valid judgement, and if it did not, it would lose its meaning and be indistinguishable from a merely personal opinion. This is in no way affected by the fact that there is not universal agreement among mankind as to the content of the moral law. The point is that the *form* of the moral law—that which makes morality what it is —is that any moral judgement, in order to be a moral judgement at all, must be universally binding. The fact that there are differences as to what the ultimate moral principles are is irrelevant. Morality, *per se*, is binding, and absolutely binding. *Fiat justitia ruat coelum* expresses what this means, however justice may be understood. The desperate efforts of linguistic philosophers to explain morality away by reducing it to other terms—such as the giving of commands to oneself—are as unconvincing as they are ingenious. The attempt to 'debunk' conscience in this manner does not really come to grips with the problem at all. The whole concept of conscience for a linguistic philosopher is really nonsense, and yet even Mr. Hare cannot evade the problem of conscience enshrined in the question: 'How shall I bring up my children?'[1] The concept of moral obligation, in other words, is the rock on which the upholders of subjectivist doctrines of morals suffer shipwreck. They turn their eyes away from it and never really face it.

This is where the attack of the psychologist on the concept of conscience comes in. He, at least, does not shirk this question. He recognizes that moral obligation lies at the heart of ethics, and that if ethics is to be explained away this can be achieved only by providing a plausible account of how the idea of moral obligation arises. This Freud claimed to be able to do; and we must next turn our attention to the formidable attack which he delivered on the authority of conscience. Let us consider the account which he gives in his *New Introductory Lectures on Psycho-Analysis*. 'Psychotics are fissured and splintered structures. . . . We cannot deny them a measure of that awe with which madmen were regarded by peoples of ancient times. They have turned away from external reality, but for that very reason they know more of internal psychic reality and can tell us much that would otherwise be inaccessible to us. One group of them suffer from what we call delusions of observation. They complain to us that they suffer continually, and in their most intimate actions, from the observation of unknown powers or persons, and they have hallucinations in which they hear these persons announcing the results of

---

[1] R. M. Hare: *The Language of Morals*, p. 74.

their observations. . . . How would it be if these mad
people were right, if we all of us had an observing function
in our egos threatening us with punishment, which, in their
case, had merely become sharply separated from the ego
and had been mistakenly projected into external reality? . . .
Under the strong impression of this clinical picture I formed
the idea that the separating off of an observing function from
the rest of the ego might be a normal feature of the ego's
structure; this idea has never left me, and I was driven to
investigate the further characteristics and relations of the
function which had been separated off in this way. The
next step is soon taken. The actual content of the delusion
of observation makes it probable that the observation is
only a first step towards conviction and punishment, so
that we may guess that another activity of this function
must be what we call conscience. There is hardly anything
that we separate off from our ego so regularly as our conscience and so easily set over against it. . . . And since the
process of recognizing a thing as a separate entity involves
giving it a name of its own, I will henceforward call this
function in the ego the super-ego.'[1] Freud then goes on to
point out that in the psychosis known as melancholia 'the
super-ego has the ego at its mercy and applies the most
severe moral standards to it; indeed, it represents the whole
demands of morality, and we see all at once that our moral
sense of guilt is the expression of the tension between the
ego and the super-ego. . . . Conscience is no doubt something within us, but it has not been there from the beginning.
In this sense it is the opposite of sexuality, which is certainly
present from the very beginning of life, and is not a thing
that comes in only later. But small children are notoriously
a-moral; they have no internal inhibitions against their
pleasure-seeking impulses. The role which the super-ego
plays later in life, is at first played by an external power, by

[1] *New Introductory Lectures on Psycho-Analysis*, pp. 81 f.

parental authority. . . . The external restrictions are intro-
jected, so that the super-ego takes the place of the parental
function, and thenceforth observes, guides and threatens the
ego in just the same way as the parents acted to the child
before.'[1]

Thus Freud states with his accustomed clarity his doctrine
of the super-ego. The first point to note, in seeking to
assess the value and validity of this hypothesis, is that the
evidence which led Freud to make it was derived not from
normal or semi-normal persons, but from psychotic patients
—i.e. those who are definitely insane. It is in such persons
as these that the super-ego is most clearly seen. This should
surely suggest a warning not to take this as a pattern for
what exists in every normal person, viz. a conscience; but
Freud gives no indication that he was aware of this danger
or did anything to guard against it. Having said this, it
must be admitted that the hypothesis of the super-ego is one
of great value and has done a great deal to help us to understand human nature. It is reasonable to suppose that everybody is possessed of a super-ego, but whether or not it
comes into being in the way that Freud suggests is another
matter. Not all psychiatrists agree with Freud here. Thus,
for example, Jung derives the super-ego from the collective
unconscious.[2] In any case the crucial question is whether it
can be roundly identified with what we call conscience, i.e.
the human capacity for forming moral judgements, and
whether it can account for the sense of moral obligation
which exists in every normal individual. I suggest that the
answer is in the negative, for the following reasons.

First, there is a basic difference between the deliverances
of the super-ego and the deliverances of a developed
conscience. The super-ego rules by fear; fear of social

[1] *Ibid.*, p. 83 f.
[2] See C. G. Jung: 'The Practice of Psychotherapy' (*Collected Works*, Vol. 16,
p. 120).

disapproval and of the consequences which flow therefrom. Conscience when it is true to itself rules by love. As St. John pointed out long ago: 'Perfect love (*agape*) casteth out fear' (1 *John* 4. 18). The point can be put in another way. The super-ego operates by means of egocentric motives; conscience works by altruistic motives. To express it in yet another way, the theme of the super-ego is: 'I must'; the theme of conscience is: 'I ought.' This vital distinction can be appreciated by viewing the question from the standpoint of guilt. Guilt can be either what Dr. J. G. McKenzie has called 'realistic' or 'unrealistic.' He says: 'True realistic guilt feelings are experiences when the guilt feelings are referred to the actual wrong-doing; when responsibility is felt; when, like Augustine, the wrongdoer says "Mea culpa"; they are referred to an objective situation. Unrealistic guilt-feelings are wholly subjective; they refer to a state of mind, and not to an objective situation.'[1] Of course, as Dr. McKenzie proceeds to show, unrealistic guilt-feelings are often projected on to an objective situation; but it is the work of the psychiatrist to enable the patient to see that, in fact, they are entirely subjective. The guilt-feelings denoted by the term 'scrupulosity' are all of this kind; but they are morbid and not true guilt feelings. Thus the super-ego can make a person feel intensely guilty for no reason or for no adequate reason; and this sometimes leads to an entirely topsy-turvy scale of moral values. I once knew a man who was tortured by the sense of guilt over masturbation, but he would commit fornication without any qualms at all! What Dr. McKenzie calls 'realistic guilt' corresponds to a proportionate cause.

As a person's character develops, the influence of the super-ego should progressively become weaker and become more and more merged in, or subordinate to, conscience, until in the end it withers away. To quote Dr. McKenzie

---

[1] J. G. McKenzie: *Guilt, Its Meaning and Significance* (1962), p. 56.

again: 'Morbid guilt is always a moment in the downward thrust of repression. Contrition or true shame is the first step in the modification of the offending tendencies. It is a totally different experience from the child's feeling when he has disobeyed a prohibition, or come short of what Freud and Karin Stephen call the Ego-ideal.'[1]

We are entitled, then, to claim that the Freudian attempt to 'debunk' conscience has failed. The capacity of man to pass moral judgements on human conduct, whether his own or that of others, is not morbid. On the contrary, it is one of the most distinctive characteristics of man. Hence Christian moral theology has always insisted that a man must always obey his conscience. It is inviolable. Of course, this is entirely different from claiming, as has often been the case, that it is infallible. It is unfortunately nothing of the kind. It can and often does err through ignorance. Sometimes this ignorance is culpable, and then it is called vincible ignorance. Sometimes it is not culpable, and then the ignorance is said to be invincible. Thus we must not equate conscience with the voice of God in the soul or in the community. Rather it is the human capacity for hearing the voice of God. That is why conscience must be educated as well as obeyed, and each individual has the duty of seeing that his conscience is an enlightened conscience. Nothing that Freud or anybody else has said has undermined the validity of this position.

Conscience, then, is not 'an emotion'; but we still have to inquire why moral judgements are so frequently emotional. Thus we say that 'we feel strongly' about some moral question. We become 'heated,' 'hot under the collar,' and easily lose control of our tempers in the conduct of moral arguments. This familiar fact of experience, however, is easily explained. It is a psychological fact that emotion is experienced when action is inhibited. Take, for example,

[1] *Ibid.*, p. 42.

the case of fear. When we are 'running for our lives' we may not be conscious, or are hardly conscious, of the emotion of fear; but let some obstacle, such as a five-barred gate, suddenly appear before us and we are overcome by the emotion. Now, although the moral law is not *per se* negative, it usually first appears to us in the form of prohibitions: 'Thou shalt not.' That is perhaps partly because of the evil bias in us all, known to theologians as original sin. It is also perhaps due to the fact that all learning is by negations. We learn what x or y is by distinguishing it from a and b. For instance, suppose we are looking down a long straight road, and see an object in the distance as it slowly moves towards us. As we try to distinguish it, we first think that it is a horse, and then we think that it is a cow, finally we see that it is a man carrying a bundle of hay. Even so, do we learn what our duty is by discovering what it is not. That is why moral codes are so often negatively framed; and that is why morality commonly appears in the form of an inhibition, and, in consequence, stirs up an emotional reaction.

We must now pass on to consider a question which is bound up with the existence of conscience, and which is much to the fore at the present time, and that is the question of responsibility. One of the most significant of psychological hypotheses is the hypothesis of the unconscious mind which necessitates belief in unconscious motives. Motive is the driving power of human action. Every act, in the proper sense of the term, depends upon a motive, or, rather, several motives. A motiveless act if it can exist at all (which is doubtful) is not to be accounted an act in the full sense of the term. Since Freud unearthed the existence, or, more accurately speaking, revealed the full significance, of the unconscious, it has become plain that many of the motives which influence human conduct never enter the field of consciousness. This means that our behaviour can be governed by unconscious influences—e.g. complexes—

of which we are totally unaware. By the technique of free-association in psycho-analysis, however, they can be brought to light; then it becomes evident that they have been influencing our behaviour without our knowing it. The same evidence is provided by the phenomenon known as post-hypnotic suggestion, whereby the patient will perform actions dictated to him under hypnosis by the psycho-analyst, without recognizing this. If he is asked why he is doing this or that which has been suggested to him under hypnosis, he will invariably give a totally different and irrelevant reason.

The influence of these deliverances of psychology upon the reality of human responsibility is clearly seen in the recent legislation allowing for the existence of 'diminished responsibility.' Section 2 of the 1957 Homicide Act says: 'When a person kills or is a party to killing of another, he shall not be convicted of murder if he was suffering from such abnormality of mind (whether arising from a condition of arrested or retarded development of mind or any inherent causes induced by disease or injury) as substantially impaired his mental responsibility for his acts or omissions in doing or being a party to the killing.' That one who commits the crime of murder may be exculpated by virtue of mental disease has long been recognized in English[1] law, being allowed for by the well-known McNaghten Rules which lay it down that the defendant on a charge of murder, if he is to be acquitted, must be able to show that, at the time of committing the act, he was suffering from a defect of reason due to mental disease such that either he did not know what he was doing or did not realize that the act was wrong. The recent Homicide Act, however, is an improvement upon these Rules in that it recognizes that morbid influences may affect not only a person's cognitive

---

[1] Scottish law and the law of various other countries has for some time recognized the category of 'diminished responsibility.'

ST. AUGUSTINES COLLEGE
LIBRARY, CANTERBURY

powers but also his emotions. Thus the phrase 'mental responsibility' which occurs in this Act means that English law now recognizes mental abnormality in a way which is more in accord with modern psychological science. It does not, however, come to grips with the question which is here of primary concern to the moral theologian, viz. the question of *moral* responsibility. Psychology, as a descriptive science, can know nothing of this concept, which brings us into the field of ethics. Apart from this, however, conscience is shorn of its ultimate authority. It is, therefore, incumbent on the moral theologian to make clear exactly what he means by human responsibility, and, without attempting a full discussion of the age-long Freedom-Determinism controversy, something must be said now about this question. To be responsible for one's actions, then, means, in the first place, to be free from external compulsion. A man who signs a document at the point of a revolver is not held to be responsible for what he has signed. So far all would agree. But what of 'internal compulsion'? If a person is driven by unconscious psychological forces to perform all his actions, can he be regarded as responsible for what he does? Surely not: and yet this seems to be the direction in which some are moving to-day. Thus, for example, Lady Barbara Wootton, in a recent book, *Social Science and Social Pathology*, has written: 'Revolutionary though the prospect of abandoning the concept of responsibility may be it is clear that we are travelling steadily towards it.'[1] Yet it is surely incredible that this can be the case; for it would reduce our human life to a puppet show.

It should be clearly recognized that Determinism, whether in the psychological form or any other, is a matter of faith

---

[1] *Ibid.*, p. 251. It is surely significant that the author, writing in the Preface of her collaborators, Miss R. Chambers and Miss V. G. Seal, says: 'the writing and the sole responsibility [*sic*] of what is said are mine.'

and not of proof, and must ever remain so. It would clearly, *ex hypothesi*, not be possible to prove scientifically that the whole of a person's conduct was the inexorable result of psychological forces, insomuch that he was reduced to the level of a machine. However far the evidence might point in that direction, it could never amount to proof. Lady Wootton takes no account of this. Indeed, she deliberately evades the issue.

The advocate of the authority of conscience, however, is in greater danger from the philosopher who seeks to undermine this by arguing that the fact that we habitually make use of praise and blame, and rightly do this, provides no evidence for thinking that responsibility means, what every normal person supposes it to mean, viz. that the individual concerned could have acted otherwise in a given case. Professor Nowell-Smith, for example, argues that this is what he calls the Libertarian's error. He writes: 'The fallacy in this argument lies in supposing that, when we say "*A* could have acted otherwise," we mean that *A*, being what he was and being in the circumstances in which he was placed, could have done something other than what he did. But in fact we never do mean this; and if we believe that voluntary action is uncaused action that is only because we erroneously believe that uncaused action is a necessary condition of moral responsibility. . . . The Determinist, on the other hand, holds that the objective possibility of alternative actions is an illusion and that, if *A* in fact did *X*, then he could not have done any action incompatible with *X*. But he holds also that differences in the various causes that might have led to *X* may be of great importance and that it is in fact from the consideration of such differences that we discover the criterion by which we judge an action to be voluntary and so moral.'[1] In other words, we are being

---

[1] P. Nowell-Smith: 'Freewill and Moral Responsibility,' *Mind* (N.S.), Vol. 57 (1948), pp. 49 and 50.

told, as Professor C. A. Campbell[1] has pointed out, that to say that *A* could have acted otherwise means that if *A* had not been *A* but somebody with a different character, he could have acted otherwise—in fact, if *A* had been not *A* but *B*. Surely this is palpably false; we do not mean anything of the kind when we say that *A* could have acted otherwise. If that is what we really meant, we should say not '*A could* have acted otherwise' but '*A would* have acted otherwise,' which is entirely different.

Furthermore, it is fair to say that people do not regard responsibility as Professor Nowell-Smith does, when he argues that this means that to call an action voluntary indicates that it falls within the class of actions that are caused by characteristics that can be strengthened or inhibited by praise or blame. And (he claims) this is what we do in fact find; moral characteristics, as opposed to intellectual and physical ones, are just those which we believe to be alterable in that way. In other words, we do not punish a man because he is bad, but he is bad because we punish him! Moreover, why, according to this theory, should we blame those who are dead and gone? They are not punishable by us. It is a weak argument to maintain that we blame them because they were once like this. Moreover, why do we hold human beings responsible but animals not responsible, although we know that we can change their characters by punishment?

What, then, are the essential requirements for human responsibility? In what does it consist? We may most conveniently answer by stating in what it does not consist. In the first place, it does not mean sheer indeterminism. As Bradley pointed out long ago in a famous essay, this is the very negation of responsibility. He wrote: 'The theory (*sc.* Non-Determinism) was to save responsibility. It saves it thus. A man is responsible, *because* there was no reason why

[1] 'Is "Freewill" a Pseudo-Problem?' *Mind* (N.S.), Vol. 60 (1951), p. 453.

he should have done one thing, rather than another thing. And that man, and *only* that man, is responsible, concerning whom it is impossible for anyone, even himself, to know what in the world he will be doing next; possibly only to know what his actions are, when once they are done, and to know that they might have been the diametrical opposite. So far is such an account from saving responsibility (as we commonly understand it) that it annihilates the very conditions of it. It is the description of a person who is *not* responsible, who (if he is anything) is idiotic.'[1] As Bradley says, a person who 'is capable of anything,' as the phrase goes, is the reverse of a responsible person.

In the second place, it does not mean that 'voluntary action is uncaused action,' as Professor Nowell-Smith asserts in the quotation above. On the contrary, voluntary action is caused by the free personality choosing between two or more courses of action. We can, of course, often predict with a high degree of probability how a certain person will act; but that is because a person's choices will obviously be influenced by what we call his character. This, however, is not to say that they are rigidly determined by his character. After all, what we call the character of a person is only our estimate of the observed uniformities of his past actions and choices. But a person must be carefully distinguished from his character, in the interests of accurate thinking. An infant has no character. That is something which he has to acquire. He exists before his character. In course of time he is able to exercise deliberate choice, and the result of these choices playing upon his temperament (his physiological inheritance) and his disposition (his acquired psychological attitudes) is to produce what we call his character, which, of course, is growing, or at any rate

[1] F. H. Bradley, *Ethical Studies*, p. 12.

changing all the time. There should really be no difficulty in appreciating this. For what we call natural causation is no more than the result of our observation of regular sequences in nature. Plato tells us he learned from Socrates that this is something entirely different from true causation. In a famous passage he says (telling us of the disappointment with which Socrates, his master, listened to Anaxagoras): 'What expectations I had formed, and how grievously was I disappointed! As I proceeded I found my philosopher altogether forsaking mind or any other principle of order, and having recourse to air, and ether, and water, and other eccentricities. I might compare him to a person who began by maintaining generally that mind is the cause of the actions of Socrates, but who, when he endeavoured to explain the causes of my several actions in detail, went on to show that I sit here because my body is made up of bones and muscles; and the bones, as he would say, are hard and have joints which divide them, and the muscles are elastic and they cover the bones, which have also a covering or environment of flesh and skin which contains them; and, as the bones are lifted at their joints by the contraction or relaxation of the muscles, I am able to bend my limbs, and this is why I am sitting here in a curved posture—that is what he would say; and he would have a similar explanation of my talking to you, which he would attribute to sound, and air and hearing, and he would assign ten thousand other causes of the same sort, forgetting to mention the true cause, which is, that the Athenians have thought fit to condemn me, and accordingly I have thought it better and more right to remain here and undergo my sentence; for I am inclined to think that these muscles and bones of mine would have gone off long ago to Megara or Boeotia—by the dog they would, if they had been moved only by their own idea of what was best, and if I had not chosen the nobler and better part, instead of playing truant and running away, of enduring any punishment which the state inflicts. There is surely a strange confusion of causes and conditions in all this.'[1] This being the case —and it is difficult to deny—it is surely paradoxical in the extreme to try to explain human willing and choosing—a kind of causation of which we all have first-hand knowledge every time we perform a deliberate action—by means of something which is entirely mysterious, viz. physical causation. Moral choice is the exercise of this power in obedience to the sense of duty. Such is moral responsibility.

[1] Plato: *Phaedo* 98 c. (Jowett's translation).

CHAPTER 6

SIN, FORGIVENESS AND ABSOLUTION

SIN is a theological term. It does not occur in books on ethics. All sin is an offence against Almighty God, the Maker and Creator of all persons and things. When we sin against our neighbours or against ourselves, therefore, at the same time we sin against the Creator to whom all creatures belong. In the language of the Old Testament, sin is 'doing evil in the sight of the Lord' (2 *Kings* 15. 18). Broadly speaking, we may say that sin may be regarded from three different points of view: (*a*) from the physical, or medical point of view; (*b*) from the legal point of view; (*c*) from the personal point of view.

(*a*) The physical point of view goes back into Old Testament times, and to the Jewish doctrine of the *yetzer hara*, or evil impulse, alleged by the rabbis to have been implanted by the Creator at birth in every human soul, this being their interpretation of Genesis 6. 5: 'And the Lord saw that the wickedness of man was great in the earth, and that every imagination of the thoughts of his heart was only evil continually.' This evil impulse was believed to have been inserted in order to provide man with the occasion of self-discipline and self-conquest. There are traces of this doctrine to be found in St. Paul's doctrine of 'the flesh' as the seat of sin. N. P. Williams wrote: 'There can be no doubt that St. Paul considers our physical nature to be the home and seat of transmitted sinfulness, though this must not be pressed to the point of attributing a Manichaean dualism between flesh and spirit to him.'[1] This is surely a self-contradictory judgement? If the flesh is *per se* the seat of human sin, that

---

[1] *A New Commentary on Holy Scripture*, Commentary on Romans 7. 15-23.

is dualism; and no Christian can accept that. Dorner said
that for St. Paul the flesh denotes 'man's entire life so far as
it is not determined by the Spirit of God.'[1] Perhaps that is
the nearest that we can get to a right understanding of the
Apostle. In this case, his conception of 'the flesh' will be
analogous to St. John's conception of 'the world' as 'society
organized apart from God.'

However this may be, the Pauline doctrine of the 'flesh'
led Tertullian and Augustine after him to a doctrine of
concupiscence which at times was certainly dualistic.

In modern times we find a similar physical doctrine of sin
espoused by Tennant in his doctrine of original sin as the
survival in man of the ape and of the tiger. Nor is there any
doubt, as Grensted pointed out in his Bampton Lectures,
that this materialistic conception of sin characterizes a good
deal of modern psychiatry. He wrote: 'The problem for the
psychologist of this latter type is that of making a clear
distinction between sin proper and conditions in which
moral freedom is in abeyance.... In ordinary psychological
practice the distinction is usually ignored. The sinful acts
and habits with which moral theology is concerned are for
the psychiatrist symptoms of a disorder to be treated on
scientific lines and their moral status is a secondary matter.
It is urged, not without reason, that the distinction between
habitual sins and cases of an undoubtedly pathological type
may be possible in theory, but is completely unworkable
when it comes to treatment.'[2] Nevertheless, there is one
insuperable objection to this way of regarding sin. It is
that sin is at root *spiritual*, not physical. William Temple
pointed this out with utmost clarity. He said: 'The centre
of trouble is not the turbulent appetites, though they are
troublesome enough, and the human faculty for imagination
increases their turbulence. But the centre of trouble is the

---

[1] Quoted in article on 'Sin,' Hastings *Dictionary of the Bible*, III, p. 535.
[2] L. W. Grensted: *Psychology and God* (1930), p. 143.

personality as a whole, which is self-centred and can only be wholesome and healthy if it is God-centred. This whole personality in action is the will; and it is the will which is perverted. Our primary need is not to control our passions by our purpose, but to direct our purpose itself to the right end.'[1] We must reject the physical doctrine of sin *in toto* as entirely false and misleading.

(*b*) This brings us to the second way of looking at sin, viz. as the infringement of law. That this must be recognized as valid can hardly be denied in the light of the New Testament. St. John says roundly: 'Sin is lawlessness' (1 *John* 3. 4). Bishop Westcott, commenting on this, says: 'The description is absolutely exhaustive. Man is constituted with a threefold relation, a threefold obligation to self, to the world, to God. To violate "law" by which this relation is defined in life is "to sin." Each conscious act by which the law is broken is "a sin"; the principle which finds expression in the special acts is "sin." When traced back to its last form this "sin" is the self-assertion of the finite in violation of the limits which guide the harmonious fulfilment of the idea of its being. Every such act, being in its essence self-regarding, self-centred, must be a violation of "love." Thus lawlessness is, under another aspect, selfishness; or as it is characterized by St. John, "hatred" in opposition to love (1 *John* 2. 9; 3. 14 ff.; 4. 20). There can be essentially no middle term.'[2] Moreover, St. Paul, despite his emphasis on the contrast between the Jewish Law and Grace has no doubts that 'the law is holy, and the commandment holy, righteous and good' (*Rom.* 7. 12). And when he says, 'I had not known sin, except through the law,' he is in effect saying the same as St. John: that sin in lawlessness. Nor does our Lord himself, for all his dislike of the 'legalism' of the Pharisees, say anything against the idea of law. When asked: 'What

---

[1] W. Temple: *Nature, Man and God*, p. 367.
[2] *Commentary on the Epistles of St. John*, pp. 37 and 38.

commandment is the first of all?' he does not say as he
might have said, and what according to the ideas of some
Christians apparently he ought to have said, 'You must not
think of goodness in this legal fashion.' He cites the first
Commandment in its Deuteronomic form (*Mark* 12. 28–31).
Moreover, in his teaching about sin, he speaks of it as a
debt to God—i.e. in legal terms (*Matt.* 6. 12; *Luke* 11. 4).
As we shall see presently, he thinks of forgiveness in terms
of the remission of a debt (*Matt.* 18. 21–35). It is, therefore,
not surprising that when Christianity came under the
influence of Roman law, this way of looking at wrongdoing
prevailed. By the time we come to Aquinas, and long before
that, sin is understood to be transgression of the eternal law
of God.[1] And ever since Aquinas moral theology has been
developed from this standpoint. That it has dangers—even
great dangers—is not to be doubted; but that it can be dis-
regarded, and moral theology become entirely independent
of it, is more than can be said.

(*c*) The third approach to the understanding of sin is the
personal. This is the most profound of all. Here is the heart
of the matter. 'Against thee only have I sinned and done
this evil in thy sight' (*Ps.* 51. 4). 'I will arise and go unto
my father, and say unto him, Father, I have sinned' (*Luke*
15. 18). 'God be merciful to me a sinner' (*Luke* 18. 13).
These are the veridical expressions of repentance, and all
Christians recognize them to be such. Sin is a turning away
from God. Contrariwise, repentance is a turning back to
God—a *returning*. This is the Biblical conception from Old
Testament times onwards. To repent is to turn (*Shubh*). It
is the greatness of the Hebrew tradition that it firmly grasped
this truth. Thus sin alienates man from God. It erects a
barrier between them (*Isa.* 59. 2). It is first, last and all the
time a personal relationship; and once this is forgotten or
ignored it loses its real meaning. Sin is not ultimately a

[1] S.T. Ia–IIae., Q. 71.

failure to reach such and such a standard, or a defilement of the soul, or a species of self-inhibition. It is disloyalty and disobedience to the living God. That is why there is only one remedy for sin; it must be forgiven.

What, then, is forgiveness? Forgiveness means reconciliation; it is a mutual process between two persons. We really require two words to express what it means, viz. forgivingness and forgiveness. When forgivingness meets sorrow for having offended—in other words, repentance—forgiveness results. This does not mean the wiping out of the past. This is impossible. But the meaning of the past can be *changed* by what follows. A misfortune can befall two persons alike. On one of them it has the effect of making him an embittered man for the rest of his life. On the other, it has the effect of making him more unselfish and determined to prevent, so far as it lies in his power, a similar misfortune befalling others. So in the case of forgiveness. Once a wrong done against another has been truly forgiven, the result of the quarrel is only to deepen and strengthen the friendship. But this does not necessarily involve the remission of the penalty. Indeed, in some form there is always the price to be paid. If one strikes another in a fit of anger, and the result is the loss of an eye, although the offence may be completely and utterly forgiven, the blinded eye remains. When the prodigal son wasted his father's substance in riotous living, and he returned home in penitence and received forgiveness, the money that he had wasted was all spent, and it may have been that his own health was permanently impaired. These things could not be undone.

That is because Nature, operating by the law of cause and effect, knows no forgiveness. In this respect it is true that as we make our bed so we must lie in it. If it were not so, the business of life could not continue. Nature must be uniform and consistent in her working. Human life, as we know it, would otherwise be impossible. 'Where the tree falleth, there shall it be' (*Eccles.* 11. 3). Thus there is the price of sin to be paid at the natural level. But it also has to be paid at the level of justice. Justice is the basis of moral law. Punishment is the vindication of justice. Despite what many modern writers say, it is basically retributive, rather than deterrent or reformatory. It is not primarily deterrent, according to Christian belief, because it is immoral to use a person as a mere means to an end. Consequently, punishment cannot be essentially deterrent. Nor can it be *basically* in order to reform the offender, for the simple reason that no offender will in fact be reformed by any punishment that he may undergo, unless he recognizes that he *deserves* to be punished. Otherwise his punishment will serve not to reform him but to embitter him. Thus at the moral level punishment is the payment of the price of sin. Moreover, because this is the case, forgiveness is not, as is sometimes alleged, immoral. The price must always be paid 'to the uttermost farthing.'

It is here, however, that we reach one of the most mysterious aspects of forgiveness. The price of sin can be paid in two different ways. It can be paid by the offender himself, or it can be paid vicariously by another. And this is the mystery, which, however mysterious, is a common fact of experience; when the price *is* paid vicariously *and willingly* by another, the offender is most likely to be brought to repentance. He may harden his heart in resistance to the most dire threats and penalties of the law; but when he sees the price of his misdeeds being patiently and willingly paid by another, his resistance is broken down. He is led to repentance. Experience shows that this is true. Let a simple tale exemplify this. Little John is an incorrigible child, swept by storms of selfish temper. He seems to be incapable of love to anyone. His parents can do nothing with him. But so far as his selfish little heart knows love at all, it is directed towards Tim, his wire-haired terrier. He has been teaching the dog a trick. The dog was slow to learn, and John in a temper kicks it in the mouth. The little dog, with its tongue red with its own blood, licks its master's hand. John, who has taken innumerable 'lickings' unmoved, cannot take this one. He runs indoors to his mother, and cries out: 'Mummy, I've been a bad boy.'

Thus far we have been discussing the question of forgiveness as between man and man. But as between man and God, how then? When man sins against God, against the moral law written in his conscience (*Rom.* 2. 14 & 15), he becomes aware of what is called 'a guilty conscience.' How can he get rid of that? One thing seems to be reasonably certain. He cannot forgive himself. Although he may try to do this, and millions do try, he is never completely successful, as the ancient Greeks knew full well, with their doctrine of the avenging Erinys, whose power reached even beyond the grave. Only God can relieve a guilty conscience; only God can forgive sins. But how can this be?

In the Scriptures, it was the teaching of the Old Testament that for deliberate sin—sin 'with a high hand' (*Num.* 15. 30) —there was no forgiveness. This was possible, it was held, only for sins of inadvertence or for ceremonial offences. But in the New Testament all that was changed. Our Lord taught that God is ready and waiting to forgive man for everything, if only he will repent. Repentance was no new conception. In Hebrew idiom it meant 'returning,' i.e. 'turning round' and going back to God. When the Prodigal said, 'I will arise and go unto my father,' he was using the Hebrew idiom which would be familiar to all our Lord's hearers. But what would not have been familiar was the picture of God going out to meet him. That was new, and that was the good news of the Gospel.

If this is the case, it may be asked, Why, then, is there any need for the atoning death of Christ in order that man may be forgiven? If all that he has to do is to repent, as the

parable of the Prodigal Son suggests, how can it be true that
our Lord died for the remission of sins? The point was put
forward by Rashdall in his Bampton Lectures. He wrote:
'Forgiveness, then, according to Jesus, follows immediately
upon repentance. No other "condition of salvation," to
use the term of later theology, has to be fulfilled. There is
not the slightest suggestion that anything else but repentance
is necessary—the actual death of a Saviour, belief in the
atoning efficacy of that death or in any other article of
faith.'[1] Apart altogether from the parts of our Lord's
teaching which speak of the atoning power of his coming
death—passages which Rashdall has to try to explain away—
this is altogether too superficial an understanding of the
nature of sin and forgiveness. It overlooks the fact that
somebody must always pay the price of sin. We have
already drawn attention to the fact that the Prodigal had to
pay part of this price himself. But there can be no doubt
that by far the greater part had to be paid by his father.
We do not need great imagination to realize how greatly
he must have suffered during the boy's absence. And when
he returned and looked once more into his father's loving
face, he could read in the furrowed lines which were not
there before he went away, and in the hair prematurely
grey, the story of that suffering. To suppose that all that
was required for him to be forgiven was for him to say
'I'm sorry' and for the father to say 'That's all right, my
boy,' as if nothing much had happened, is to misread the
meaning of the story from beginning to end. It is crystal
clear that there was a big price to be paid in that episode,
and the greater part was paid vicariously.

Read in this way, the story does not make the need for
the Atoning sacrifice of Christ appear unnecessary. The
reverse is the case. It clearly indicates that the price of sin
must be paid vicariously. It also reveals most clearly what

[1] H. Rashdall: *The Idea of Atonement in Christian Theology* (1920), p. 26.

our experience teaches us also, that when that price is paid vicariously it becomes redemptive. The boy may have said while he was still in the far country, 'I will arise . . . and say, Father, I have sinned'; but it would all have been in vain if his father had not in the meantime been paying the price of his sin, and consequently been ready to receive him with open arms on his return.

The parable of the Prodigal Son is a story which deals with the problem of sin as it affects individuals, and shows how the price must be paid before they can be reconciled. We have to remember, however, that the sin of the world is a 'massa peccati,' as Augustine saw, which cannot be laid at the door of this individual or of that. The sin of the world is different from the sins of the world. In other words, it is more than the sum total of the offences for which individuals are responsible. To put it in another way, there is a corporate as well as an individual aspect of sin. There is, for example, the hideous sin of war. The blame for any particular war cannot be laid entirely on the shoulders of politicians, or even of dictators, although they may be primarily to blame. War, like other great social evils, is the result of the corporate sin of the human race. Somebody has to pay the price of this. Christians believe that, in some mysterious way, our Lord did just this, and thereby established a new relationship between God and man. In the unspeakable agony of his last hours upon the Cross, when the darkness enfolded him, and he experienced the sense of separation from the Father, he was bearing the sin of the world.

We now come to the theology of Absolution. There are here two entirely different doctrines which we must consider. The first is that priestly absolution is a sacrament and that it confers the forgiveness of sins. We find this fully developed by Aquinas. The form of this sacrament, according to St. Thomas, consists in the words *Ego te absolvo*. He argues that, although these actual words were not given us by Christ, they are implied in the words spoken by him to St. Peter immediately after his confession: 'Whatsoever thou shalt bind on earth shall be bound in heaven' (*Matt.* 16. 19). He maintains that the precatory forms of absolution to be found in the public offices of the Church are to be understood simply as prayers for forgiveness on behalf of others.[1] Furthermore he argues that penance is a sacrament and that since sacraments do that which they signify (*efficiunt quod figurant*) it necessarily follows that this must be the effect of absolution. Aquinas meets the objection that penance cannot be a sacrament because it has no outward material form by arguing that in this instance the material of the sacrament is constituted by the human acts involved, as is the case with holy matrimony when the material of the sacrament is the contract made by the parties. It must be admitted, however, that his argument to prove that penance is a sacrament is extremely weak. It is as follows: Baptism is regarded as a purification from sin and so is penance. That is why St. Peter said to Simon: 'Do penance for this thy sin.' But baptism is acknowledged to be a sacrament; the same must therefore hold good of penance. The point, however, is not of first importance except for establishing the traditional number of seven sacraments. However this may be, penance is clearly sacramental. It has 'the nature of a sacrament,' to use the phrase employed in another con-nexion in the Thirty-nine Articles, even though it might be held that it is not 'a sacrament of the Gospel.'

Aquinas then proceeds to argue that penance is necessary for salvation, which, of course, is a very different matter. He bases this teaching on the dubious interpretation of the Vulgate version of our Lord's words: 'If you have not penance, you shall all likewise perish' (*Luke* 13. 3). Aquinas

[1] S.T. III. Q. 4. a. 3.

then draws a distinction between what is absolutely neces-sary and what is conditionally necessary for salvation. Baptism and the grace of Christ, he says, are absolutely necessary for salvation; but penance is not like that. It is necessary only for those who are subject to sin, quoting the words in The Prayer of Manasses: 'Thou, therefore, O Lord, who art the God of the just, hast not appointed repentance to the just, to Abraham, and Isaac, and Jacob, who have not sinned against thee' (ver. 4). He then imme-diately proceeds to quote the words of St. James to the effect that sin in the end leads to death (*Jas.* 1. 15). Sin, therefore, must be removed by the sacrament of penance where the virtue of Christ's passion is operative by the absolution of the priest together with the penitence of the penitent.[1]

In this teaching we can see the influence of the Fourth Lateran Council of 1215, requiring annual confession of all the faithful. As Moberly said, the mediaeval theology of penance was based on the required practice instead of the practice being based on a sound theology.[2] It was, therefore, necessary for Aquinas to show that confession before a priest was essential, and why forgiveness without it was ordinarily impossible. It is important, however, to bear in mind that this position was modified by the Council of Trent, which taught that perfect contrition reconciles the sinner to God without the sacrament of penance, provided that there is present the desire to receive the sacrament, because it has been enjoined by the Church.[3]

It follows, therefore, that, if the requirement of 1215 does not possess ecumenical authority—and the basis of the Anglican position is that it does not—perfect penitence will lead to forgiveness apart from the sacrament. This has been

[1] *Op. cit.* a. 5.
[2] R. C. Moberly in Fulham Conference on Confession (1901), quoted in Art. 'Repentance,' *Prayer Book Dictionary*, p. 606.
[3] Conc. Trid. Sessio XIV.

the general Anglican teaching. It does not, however, follow from this that absolution is a purely judicial and declaratory act which indicates a *fait accompli*, as, for instance, Hooker argues.

This brings us to the second of the two doctrines of absolution to which we referred. According to this, absolution does no more than 'ascertain us of God's most gracious and merciful pardon'[1] in relation to God, although in relation to the Church it brings release from ecclesiastical discipline. 'As for the ministerial sentence of private absolution, it can be no more than a declaration of what God hath done; it hath but the force of the prophet Nathan's absolution, "God hath taken away thy sin" than which construction, especially of words judicial, there is not anything more vulgar.'[2]

In arguing for this, however, Hooker is driven to adopt a most unsatisfactory position. He maintains that, if it is true that perfect contrition brings forgiveness, there is nothing for the sacrament of penance to do but to declare and ratify a *fait accompli*, 'seeing no man can be a true penitent or contrite which doth not both love God and sincerely abhor sin.'[3] In saying this, however, Hooker blurs a vital distinction between sincere penitence and perfect penitence. The fact is that the more truly penitent a person is, the more is he led to realize the imperfection of his penitence. This may be paradoxical, but it is a fact of experience. Indeed, as Moberly argues forcibly in his book *Atonement and Personality*, in order to dissociate oneself completely from one's sin—and this is what penitence is—one would have to be without sin. Thus our Lord is the only perfect penitent.

It follows from this that since the sincerely penitent person may be led to doubt the reality of his penitence, 'the benefit of absolution' must be that it makes good this felt deficiency, thus conferring fullness of forgiveness as the basis of the full

[1] E.P. VI. 6. 4.   [2] *Ibid.*, VI. 6. 8.   [3] *Ibid.*, VI. 6. 12.

assurance of forgiveness. In other words, the purely declaratory doctrine of absolution breaks down at the critical point. It cannot bring certain relief to the doubtful or the distressed conscience. That can come only if the penitent is assured that the grace of absolution makes good the deficiency of his own contrition; if, that is to say, it not only declares him to be forgiven but also renders it possible. Indeed, on the purely declaratory doctrine of absolution, we are ultimately driven to a Pelagian position; for in a sense we earn our forgiveness by our own perfect contrition on that view. The truth is that, apart from the grace of Christ, we cannot repent; and the more sincerely we do repent the more are we likely to realize our sore need of the grace of absolution.

We have quoted Hooker as an exponent of the declaratory doctrine of absolution; but it must not be supposed that this is necessarily the Anglican doctrine. Other theologians of eminence can be quoted on the other side. It will suffice to quote Bishop Andrewes and Bishop Hall. The former in his sermon on absolution says, speaking from the text, 'Whatsoever sins ye remit, they are remitted unto them': 'For Christ hath not thus indited it: "Whose sins ye wish or ye pray for" or, "Whose sins ye declare to be remitted"; but "whose sins ye remit"; using no other word in the Apostles' than he useth in his own. And to all these, in St. Matthew, he addeth his solemn protestation of "Verily, verily"; or, "Amen, Amen," that so it is and shall be. And all to certify us that he fully meaneth with effect to ratify in heaven that is done on earth, to the sure and steadfast comfort of them that shall partake it.'[1] Bishop Hall deals with the following case of conscience. Case IX. 'Whether I need, in case of some foul sin committed by me, to have recourse to God's Minister for absolution; and what effect I may expect therefrom?' After discussing the circumstances

[1] Sermon on Absolution.

which might lead a person to make his confession, he deals with the nature of the absolution. He writes: 'Yet, withal, it must be yielded that the blessed Son of God spake not those words of his last commission in vain: "Whosesoever sins ye remit, they are remitted unto them; and whosesoever sins ye retain, they are retained": neither were they spoken to the then present apostles only, but, in them, to all their faithful successors to the end of the world. It cannot, therefore, but be granted, that there is some kind of power left in the hand of Christ's ministers both to remit and to retain sin.

'Neither is this power given only to the governors of the Church, in relation to the censures to be inflicted or relaxed by them; but to all God's faithful ministers, in relation to the sins of men; a power not sovereign and absolute, but limited and ministerial; for either quieting the conscience of the penitent, or further aggravating the conscience of sin and terror of judgement to the obstinate and rebellious. Neither is this only by way of a bare verbal declaration' which might proceed from any other lips; but in the way of an operative and effectual application, by virtue of that delegate or commissionary authority, which is by Christ entrusted with them.'[1]

What, then, are we to understand by the grace of absolution? First, it would seem that persons cannot be absolved collectively; for even if the purely declaratory doctrine of absolution be true, the minister cannot declare anyone absolved unless and until he is in a position to judge of his or her penitence. This means that absolution must be given to individuals. The absolutions given in the public services of the Church are, therefore, to be understood simply as prayers for the forgiveness of sinners, thus being generically different from sacramental absolution.

[1] *Works*, VII, p. 122.

Secondly, the benefit of absolution is an operation of divine grace whereby all the defects in the penitence of the penitents are made good by the merits of our Lord's passion applied individually to this or that individual. We have seen that, unless this is the case, 'the benefit of absolution' may fail entirely to ease the troubled conscience, which easement, even on the purely declaratory theory, is the purpose of the rite. This brings absolution into line with the other sacraments as they are understood by Catholic theology: *efficiunt quod figurant*. In other words, absolution is not merely a sign of God's forgiveness, but, in the language of the Thirty-nine Articles, an 'efficacious sign.'

CHAPTER 7

A MORALITY OF INSPIRATION OR A MORALITY OF ENDS?

TRADITIONAL moral theology, as we have seen, has an Aristotelian basis. 'The Philosopher,' as Aquinas habitually calls Aristotle, builds his ethical teaching on the thesis that every act depends upon a chosen end. There is, in human life, a scale of ends. The lesser ends are what we call 'means,' as, for instance, we choose a pen as a means of writing. Again, we write for a purpose—a letter or a book. Yet again, we write the letter or the book for a further purpose, and so on. Ultimately, however, we come to a final end or purpose, or, if not to one single end or purpose, to a limited number of regulative purposes, which are self-evidently reasonable to every normal human being. Undemonstrated principles, according to Aristotle, govern all scientific thought. They also govern human conduct. Thus everybody assumes without argument that behaviour which promotes the end of human happiness is reasonable and good. Ethics, therefore, is concerned with the pursuit of the good, in accordance with nature, for 'in the sphere of nature all things are arranged in the best possible way.'[1] But, whereas Aristotle had thought of ethics as a part of politics, concerned solely with our life here, Aquinas lifts it up to the enjoyment of our supernatural End which is the Vision of God—a transition rendered easy by reason of the fact that Aristotle had taught that contemplation is the noblest activity in our life here on earth.

We have seen that this approach to morals is being widely questioned to-day. It is argued that it is unsatisfactory to base morals on *a priori* ends. We must rather base it on

[1] *Nicomachaean Ethics*, 1099 b.

practical experience. We have already considered some of
the limitations of the empirical approach in morals; but the
matter demands further consideration, in view of the fact
that the Christian ethic is avowedly an ethic of the Holy
Spirit—i.e. an ethic of inspiration. This introduces two
factors of which careful account must be taken: (*a*) the Holy
Spirit leads the Church, as the Spirit-bearing Body of
Christ, *progressively* into all truth. So our Lord had taught.
(*b*) This links up with a second factor, which is that changing
circumstances bring to light new moral problems. The
acquisition of the power to control atomic energy, the
discovery of the art of artificial insemination, new techniques
in human sterilization and contraception, give rise to familiar
examples of such new problems. It is possible that, before
long, we shall have acquired the power to determine the
sex of an unborn foetus, thus creating still another major
moral problem.

According to the traditional approach all these problems,
and any others which may arise, can be treated, and must be
treated, from the standpoint that morality is governed by
the pursuit of certain natural ends. Consequently conduct
which contravenes those ends must be condemned as sinful.
Thus, for instance, it is natural for man, who is governed by
the 'instinct' of self-preservation, to preserve his life. Suicide,
therefore, is unnatural, contrary to the will of the Creator
and to be condemned. In like manner, sterilization is an
unnatural mutilation of the human body and is legitimate
only if designed for the good of the body as a whole, even
as amputation of a limb might be. This teaching is clearly
set forth in the Encyclical of Pius XI *Casti Connubii*: 'Christian doctrine establishes and the light of human reason makes
it most clear, that private individuals have no power over
the members of their bodies than that which pertains to their
natural ends; and they are not free to destroy or mutilate
their members, or in any other way render themselves unfit

for their natural functions, except when no other provision can be made for the good of the whole body.'

Much modern Christian thought has reacted against this position. It stands to reason that one who does not accept the theistic background to Nature will not accept such teaching; but even those who do may hesitate to accept it in some cases. Thus Mr. G. F. Woods writes:[1] 'Even when the ethics of naturalism are resisted, those who believe in a natural moral law find it difficult to discriminate between what is natural and what is unnatural. Is, for instance, family planning natural or unnatural? And, if we do not know what is natural, why should we do what is natural? In what sense does the natural world include both what is the case and what ought to be the case? Can any natural fact or facts be the ground of the distinction between right and wrong? How can we use the word "natural" in any clear sense if we are not clear what we mean by "Nature"? I mention these points and questions in passing, only to show that the tradition of Natural Law as a guide to right living is somewhat puzzling.' But he goes on to say: 'We ought not hastily to discard an instrument as useless because it is hard to use and may be misused.' In any case, it is argued by some Christian writers that Supernature rather than Nature should be our guide, the former as revealed to us by the Holy Spirit in the changing circumstance of life.

The case of human sterilization provides a convenient example by which to illustrate this modern reaction of which we have been speaking. It is indicated by what is said in the recent *Report on Sterilisation*[2] drawn up by members of the Church of England. The authors of this Report say: 'To work both from principles and empirically at the

---

[1] In *Soundings* ed. A. R. Vidler (1962), p. 202.

[2] *Sterilisation: an Ethical Inquiry*, published for the Church Assembly Board for Social Responsibility (1962).

same time is no easy task; it is one to be undertaken, nevertheless.'[1] They proceed to say later on: 'When the grounds
of this discussion were first laid down, sterilization was not
known as a surgical possibility except as a consequence of
castration; traditional moral theology was not called upon
to consider sterilization apart from castration, as we are now.
Secondly, the command "Be fruitful, and multiply and
replenish the earth" was given when the utmost fruitfulness
was a social necessity; and throughout the centuries the
"quiverful" of children were social as well as spiritual blessings
in the long, long campaign to cultivate virgin forest and
soil and to replace the ravage of war, pestilence and disease.
Traditional moral theology has not been called upon to
consider the extent of the obligations of parenthood under
the threat of over-population. We are discussing something
new in Christian history; our task is to consider this new
situation in the light of established principles. . . .

'Faced as we are by a situation in which a responsible
government is pursuing, together with other ameliorative
measures, a policy of persuasion for voluntary sterilization,
and asked by Christian doctors and nurses involved in the
carrying out of this policy for help in deciding for themselves how far they can co-operate, we are bound to conclude
that we find no grounds on which to reply in terms of an
absolute negative. The Church of England does not claim
to be infallible and it may err. But it does believe in progressive revelation under the guidance of the Holy Spirit.
And we believe that light on this question is slowly dawning,
and we are prepared tentatively to express the opinion that
there are circumstances in which an operation for sterilization
may legitimately be employed.'[2]

In considering this question, the committee state that they
are not primarily concerned with the 'therapeutic, eugenic
and punitive use of sterilization' but mainly with sterilization

[1] *Ibid.*, p. 19.   [2] *Ibid.*, pp. 24 and 25.

as a contraceptive device. In reaching their conclusions they are influenced by two factors in the contemporary situation over and above the alleged dangers of over-population. The first is that for multitudes in the circumstances in which they have to live 'sexual abstinence is out of the question' as a means of population control. They proceed to say: 'It is not morally eligible for the moralist to enunciate a formula which, however orthodox and conclusive it may appear to him, is yet demonstrably beyond the capacity of most of the people whom he would require to live by it.' One might suppose that they had never heard of the grace of God. Indeed, one of the most surprising features in this discussion is that no distinction is drawn between the conduct of the Christian and that of the non-Christian. It is, moreover, surely irrelevant to the validity of a moral principle to estimate it according to the capacity of the majority to fulfil it. Thus, for example, it is probably the case that the majority of persons in the world are unable consistently to speak the truth, but this makes no difference to the fact that it is wrong, in general, not to speak the truth.

The second factor which has influenced the signatories of this Report is that sterilization is now, at least in some cases, a reversible process. In so far as this is so, sterilization as a contraceptive measure comes into line with other contraceptive devices. It is admitted, however, that it would be 'unfair as yet' to allow 'too heavy a reliance upon the reversibility of male sterilization. . . . It might require great determination for a man to secure a successful reversal of a vasectomy.'[1]

What, then, is the upshot of this empirical approach to the use of sterilization as a contraceptive device? Has the fresh evidence afforded by the recent changed circumstances given ground for a reversal of the traditional judgement based on the unlawfulness of mutilating the human body

[1] *Ibid.*, p. 22.

H

except in case of necessity for its good as a whole? The core of the modern argument is that it is wrong to make the well-being of the body of the individual the sole ground of the judgement. The well-being of society as a whole must be taken into account in the face of the threat of over-population. Yet in fact we find the argument conducted not simply in the context of the 'teeming millions of the East' where starvation threatens, but in the context of any family anywhere. We are told: 'It follows that husband and wife will consider first the size of their present family; whether, in a culture which so requires, there are in it an acceptable number of boys, allowing for the normal hazards of disease and death; whether, in their judgement of their economic resources, they are distinguishing clearly between on the one hand the necessities of life and its legitimate social and educational opportunities, and, on the other, desirable but dispensable luxuries and unrealistic ambitions.'[1] We seem to have moved a long way from the traditional requirement of necessity which earlier had been stated to be 'the key-word in this discussion.'[2]

The question which ultimately faces us, then, is this: Have we good reason for saying that the moral judgement that the use of sterilization as a contraceptive device is in accordance with the mind of the Holy Spirit rather than the traditional judgement that it is sinful because unnatural to mutilate the human body except under the pressure of necessity for preserving it?

We have already seen that one great difficulty in the empirical approach to morals is that we are ultimately forced back to first principles, which we cannot reach empirically. No amount of experimenting or consideration of changing circumstances can enable us to discover what these principles are, or disclose to us the mind of the Spirit. It would seem that before we can venture to claim the mind

[1] *Ibid.*, p. 30.   [2] *Ibid.*, p. 17.

of the Spirit for any course of action we must at least find
something approximating to a unanimous moral judgement
of the Church as a whole. Hitherto that judgement in
respect of sterilization has been that it is sinful because unnatural to mutilate the human body except to preserve it.
It is clear that we are very far from being in a position at
present to say that this judgement has been overthrown. In
this matter, at least, the ethic of inspiration coincides with the
ethic of ends.

We now turn to another practical moral problem in
which the empirical approach is being canvassed with a
view to modifying, if not overthrowing, traditional Christian morality, viz. the problem of homosexuality. Thus,
for example, we read in the recently published pamphlet,
Towards a Quaker View of Sex: 'We have no hesitation in
taking every now and then an empirical approach—to ask
for instance whether homosexual contacts are really "unnatural" or repulsive.'[1] Later on the authors of this pamphlet
quote with approval the statement of the Wolfenden Committee on homosexuality questioning the commonly held
belief that homosexual conduct leads to the demoralization
and decay of civilization, and they go on to say: 'We should
go further, and question whether a feeling of revulsion,
however strongly felt, is an adequate ground for moral
censure.'[2]

It is interesting to observe that this appeal to empiricism
is somewhat hesitating; moreover, the authors of this
pamphlet also appeal to nature when they argue that it is
questionable whether homosexual practices *are* 'unnatural.'
Indeed, in another passage they put forward the argument
that 'homosexuality is natural' for those members of the
male sex for whom 'a happy sexual relationship with a
woman is not possible.'[3] Yet if we are really going to adopt
an empirical approach to this question, the widespread

[1] *Op. cit.*, p. 11.   [2] *Ibid.*, p. 27.   [3] *Ibid.*, p. 21.

revulsion and disgust which is experienced by many in connexion with homosexual *practices* is certainly an empirical phenomenon and must be fairly taken into account. Clearly, not much assistance is to be found in that quarter for those who wish to validate the legitimacy of homosexual practices by empirical evidence. To ask, as the Quaker Report does, whether these practices *are* really repulsive is surely a rather meaningless question. If people find them repulsive, they *are* for such people repulsive. The empiricist here, however, thinks that he can find assistance by assessing, or trying to assess, the social consequences of an easy tolerance of these practices. As we have seen, it is being denied that there is any evidence that general toleration of homosexual practices had any great influence on the corruption and downfall of the Roman Empire. Here is another instance of the difficulty which we have consistently met in dealing with moral empiricism, viz. the difficulty of collecting and assessing the evidence.

There is, however, another quarter to which the modern empiricist is looking for guidance in dealing with this perplexing problem, and that is the evidence of modern psychiatry. This raises the difficult problem of bisexuality. Ever since Krafft-Ebing published his celebrated work, *Psychopathia Sexualis*, it has been held by some psychiatrists that the human being is bisexual, containing biologically in every case both masculine and feminine components. According to this view, in the ordinary male, the masculine elements are dominant; in the ordinary female, the feminine elements are dominant. Nevertheless, there is a large proportion of the human race in which the masculine and feminine elements are more evenly balanced, and these form what are called 'inverts' or congenital homosexuals. Furthermore, the fact that even normal individuals all have elements of the other sex in their make-up means that they all go through homosexual phases in their development, and, moreover, if these same homosexual elements are unduly stimulated in early life this may turn them into homosexuals, though not unalterably.

This teaching was taken up by Freud, Havelock Ellis and others; but it has not gone unchallenged, and the question—which is ultimately a biological question—is still under debate.[1] It is not at all certain that congenital inverts exist at all.

Some authors, however, write as if it were an empirically established fact that a considerable proportion of the human race are congenital homosexuals, and claim that since this was unknown to the fashioners of the Christian tradition this means that they were mistaken in condemning sodomy and allied practices as 'unnatural vice.' Thus, for example, Dr. S. Bailey can write: 'Here the Christian tradition affords us little guidance, for it knows only one kind of homosexual behaviour—that which would be termed "perversion"; thus to one of the most perplexing ethical problems of our time it has at best but an indirect and dubious reference.'[2] And he goes on to argue that there is 'an intrinsic difference between the acts of the pervert and those of the invert'[3] and he claims that homosexual acts on the part of a congenital invert cannot be called 'unnatural' and therefore, presumably, must not be condemned.

This criticism of tradition is entirely without empirical foundation. In the first place, as has been said, it is far from certain if congenital inverts exist at all, and, if they do, how numerous they are. Havelock Ellis's statement that they form well over one per cent[4] of the population is no more than a wild and unsubstantiated guess. But even if they do exist in quantity, that does not alter the fact that

---

[1] See, e.g., for a discussion of this matter, W. G. Cole: *Sex and Love in the Bible* (1960), pp. 353 ff.

[2] S. Bailey: *Homosexuality and the Western Christian Tradition* (1953), p. 169.

[3] *Ibid.*

[4] H. Ellis: *The Psychology of Sex* (1934), p. 207.

they are abnormal, just as (for example) those born colour-blind, though fairly numerous, are suffering from an abnormal and unnatural condition, being in fact freaks of nature. Inverts, if they exist, must be judged to be the same. As for the argument that homosexual acts committed by an 'invert' are less culpable than those of a 'pervert,' it is entirely without substance; for in either case the temptation to be resisted is equally strong, unless and until the condition has been changed by psychiatric means.

St. Paul in his famous arraignment of the pagan world in Romans I sees the homosexual indulgence of the ancient world as a symptom of its idolatrous turning away from God. He did not possess the psychological knowledge of sex which we have to-day by which we are able to recognize homosexuality *per se* as a disease rather than a sin. Yet we have no real ground for questioning the truth of his argument that homosexual practices lead men not nearer to God but away from him. It is certainly going much too far to claim that it has been shown empirically that the Christian tradition which has consistently condemned homosexual practices as evil and degrading has been mistaken. This is not, of course, to prejudge what attitude the law should adopt in this matter. It is quite possible to adhere firmly to the Christian tradition here and at the same time to deny that homosexual practices should, in general, be treated as criminal. This is a question which does not come within the province of moral theology, or concern us now.

Let us test the empirical approach by taking another example, viz. euthanasia. This takes two forms: (*a*) the taking of the life of imbeciles, mental defectives and others deemed to be useless members of society, without their permission; and (*b*) the painless ending of a human life beset by a fatal disease accompanied by extreme pain, with the permission of the patient—voluntary euthanasia. The former practice would be repudiated by the vast majority

of Christians as an infringement of the sacred rights of
human personality, and need not concern us now. The
latter practice, however, can find a good deal of support,
and there is a division among Christians concerning it. In
1936 the Voluntary Euthanasia Society was formed in this
country, and a bill legalizing euthanasia in this form was
introduced into the House of Lords, where it did not find
strong support, and it was, by leave, withdrawn. Two
years later a similar bill was introduced in U.S.A. in the
Nebraska Assembly, but it was not passed. So far no country
in the world has legalized the practice, and there is very
strong opposition to it. It is also true, however, that there
are a great many who are in favour of it.

The traditional Christian argument against euthanasia in
this form is that it is, in fact, an act of suicide, and this is
contrary to the divine law. This is not because, as Christians
are sometimes falsely asserted to hold, human life has an
absolute value, but because man holds his life in trust from
God, and has not absolute authority over it. On the other
hand, traditional Christian theology does allow two exceptions against the taking of human life. The first is in the case
of a just war, and the second is in the interests of self-defence.
Consequently the prohibition is not absolute. The moral
question, therefore, centres upon the problem whether or not
a third exception should be allowed in the case of a person
who is enduring the last agonies of a fatal and prolonged
illness. Here the traditional position is to say that it is
legitimate to administer drugs to relieve the pain, even if
they may incidentally shorten the life of the patient. The
point was clearly expressed by Pope Pius XII in 1957 in
speaking of the use of drugs to alleviate pain. He said: 'If
there exists no direct causal link, either through the will of
interested parties or by the nature of things, between the
induced unconsciousness and the shortening of life—as
would be the case if the suppression of the pain could be

obtained only through the shortening of life; and, if on the other hand, the actual administration of drugs brings about two distinct effects, the one the relief of pain, the other the shortening of life, the action is lawful. It is necessary, however, to observe whether there is, between these two effects, a reasonable proportion, and if the advantages of the one compensate for the disadvantage of the other. It is important also to ask oneself if the present state of science does not allow the same result to be obtained by other means. Finally, in the use of the drug, one should not go beyond the limits which are actually necessary.'

Thus it seems to be clear that in this instance the traditional moral theology does make allowance for empirical factors. Thus the Pope explicitly says that the relative advantages and disadvantages in the use of narcotic drugs in such circumstances should be weighed. This is an appeal to empirical evidence. But the fundamental principle of moral judgement which underlies the Pope's argument is the principle of the double effect, as the foregoing quotation indicates. Many Christian moralists, however, will think that it is much more satisfactory to deal with this problem as a choice between two evils, viz. allowing the patient to endure a lingering and agonizing death and shortening his span of life in relieving his pain. As Dr. Glanville Williams has written: 'The immediate relief of pain counterbalances the risk of accelerated death. If so much be admitted, it obviously becomes very difficult to determine when, if ever, there is an unlawful act of euthanasia in the progressive administration of the drug. The more violent and protracted the pain to be relieved, the greater the dose of the drug required to be administered, and the more the doctor is justified in ignoring the risk that this drug will immediately or indirectly bring about a curtailment of life. As the fatal illness draws to a close, with less and less remaining to the patient, risk increases, and the curtailment of life comes to be not a speculation for the future but a matter of immediate choice—a choice, perhaps, between death to-day and death next week or to-morrow. Thus a point is reached at which, proceeding upon the same principles as he has followed heretofore and which have so far been lawful, the doctor is led to give what he knows is likely to be an immediately fatal dose. It would be extremely artificial to say that this last dose, which is administered upon the same principle as all the previous ones, is alone unlawful. The fact is that there is no logical or moral chasm between what may be called shortening life and accelerating death. Once admit the principle that a physician may knowingly for sufficient reason shorten a patient's expectation of life— which cannot be denied—and one is compelled to admit that he may knowingly for sufficient reason, put an end to his patient's life immediately.'[1]

Where does this argument lead us in the moral theology of euthanasia? In the debate in the House of Lords, Lord Horder was reported as saying that the good doctor is aware of the distinction between prolonging life and prolonging the act of dying. Certainly it can be assumed that in practice most doctors do, in fact, by administration of drugs in order to deaden pain, shorten the lives of their patients. It is also safe to say that, although they have strictly no legal protection for such acts, the law winks at them. In other words, euthanasia in this form—and it cannot be denied that it is euthanasia—is generally approved on empirical grounds, even if it is difficult to defend as a matter of strict theory. It is certainly an entirely different matter from the commission of a solemn act of euthanasia expressly chosen by the patient. There can be no doubt that this would be repugnant to the conscience of a large number of physicians, perhaps the majority, and, if legalized, it might well prove harmful to the patient-doctor relationship, as well as to the

[1] Glanville Williams: *The Sanctity of Life and the Criminal Law* (1956), p. 288.

relationship of the patient and his immediate relatives. Indeed, the moral question is immediately posed whether it is right to put any dying person into the position of having to decide whether or not to end his own life in this way. It might well make a lingering last illness even more unendurable, if the patient knew that he had this legal right.

The upshot of this discussion would seem to be that, in fact, the problem of euthanasia is largely being solved empirically. It is quite clear that the alleviation of pain is regarded as a positive good by the Christian conscience. The days are long passed when 'twilight sleep' was condemned as being contrary to the divine law. On the other hand, Christians would hold that the alleviation of pain at all costs and to the harm of the spiritual condition of the patient is unlawful. He has the right and the duty to prepare himself for death so far as circumstances allow. Indeed, this is one of the reasons put forward by some of the supporters of voluntary euthanasia. Empirically, however, if that were ever to be legalized, it would probably turn out that the latter might well place many patients in such a moral dilemma as to bring added distress to their last illness. There seems to be a good deal, therefore, to be said for leaving the matter as it stands and to the good sense of the medical profession. Enthusiastic advocates of euthanasia might well ponder the testimony of Dean Inge who said that, although he did not hold euthanasia to be sinful, he himself hoped that, if he were to have to suffer a painful and lingering last illness, he would be given grace to endure to the end.

In considering the question of the guidance of the Holy Spirit, it will have been observed that we have spoken of it in terms of a corporate guidance given to the Church. It is indeed true that ultimately the conscience of each individual must guide the conduct of that individual. *Conscientia semper sequenda est,* even when it is an erring conscience. At the same time the individual member of the Church is entitled to expect guidance from the general mind of the Church. He is not *solely* dependent upon his own conscience. This is sometimes overlooked. Thus, for example, the Lambeth Conference of 1958 in its resolutions on family planning said that this must be 'in such ways as are mutually acceptable to husband and wife in Christian conscience' without giving any guidance to that conscience—a most unfortunate lapse. (Resolution 115.) To interpret the ethics of inspiration individualistically is to run counter to the facts of Christian history from the Council of Jerusalem (*Acts* 15) onwards. The guidance of the Holy Spirit is given in the first place to the Body as a whole, and only in the second place to the individual member of the Body.

It was at this point, I would submit, that a wrong turn was taken by the theologians at the Reformation; and their successors have followed them, in their approach to morals. They conceived that the question of both religion and morals was strictly between the individual soul and God. With the illumination of the Word of God each person could, and indeed, must, experience for himself the grace and guidance of God, so that he is enabled to direct his footsteps aright amid all the perplexing paths of life. There is, indeed, a Church, a Christian Community, but it consists of the collocation of all believers who have experienced individually the saving grace of God. Ultimately this community is known only to God himself. It cannot mediate for each individual ethical illumination, therefore. Nor is this necessary, for every believer has the witness in his own heart and needs nothing more.

Thus, as we have already seen, Luther's doctrine of justification by faith renders the conception of moral laws redundant, just because the ethical approach is strictly individualistic. Every believer is inspired directly by the reading of the Scriptures so that he becomes capable of knowing where his duty lies. Casuistry in any and every form becomes unnecessary. The true believer is delivered from a doubting conscience by reason of his submission to the Word of God. But this raises the all-important question: Does he in fact always manifest the most truly Christian standard of conduct? Because he has no doubts about this himself, the question is not thereby settled. In other words, Does the ethic of Luther in fact universally commend itself to the Christian conscience? It certainly has not done so in point of historical fact; nor can it be fairly equated with the standpoint of the New Testament ethic.

There is a further difficulty. The ethic of the first Reformer had no social dimension. 'Luther's over-riding concern for a personal assurance of salvation in the blessedness of inner experience, his division of spheres of human activity into the Two Realms of the Heavenly Kingdom of love and forgiveness and the Earthly Kingdom of the sword and law where power and coercion hold sway, his view that the world is the devil's inn and the human heart alone the sanctuary of God's grace, suggests a separation of the concerns of the soul from the contamination of mundane affairs. The emphasis of the German Reformer produces a piety not unconnected with religious isolationism; it has been charged with producing a social defeatism, a spiritual *laissez faire*, and abandonment of the tasks of the temporal order.'[1] In the teaching of Calvin the social reference is much stronger, but the ultimate dichotomy still remains unbridged. The light of the Gospel is still imparted to the elect individually by the Holy Spirit shining through the written Word of God.

When inspiration is understood as being given to the Holy Community in the first place, and in the second place to each individual through the Church, however, it is found that the morality of inspiration tends to approximate to the

---

[1] E. Duff: *The Social Thought of the World Council of Churches* (1956), pp. 317, 318.

morality of ends; for in fact the traditional moral theology of the Church as a morality of ends has commended itself to the mind of the Church as a whole. It has in no sense been forced upon it by authority. This fact must be borne in mind whenever a tension arises in the minds of individuals between the two.

This brings us to the consideration of the question as to what is to happen when this tension reaches breaking point, as, for instance, is happening in the case of contraceptive sterilization among Christians in India and other countries where 'over-population' is liable to the threat of famine. There can be no doubt that the arguments put forward in the Report, *Sterilisation*, do not express—at present, at least —the general mind of Christendom. What, therefore, is (say) a Christian doctor in India to do about the matter, if he remains doubtful? The answer would seem to be that he may, and indeed must, take refuge in the well-tried maxim of Christian moral theology: Of two evils choose the lesser. If so be that contraceptive sterilization is wrong, it is also true that to perform actions likely to aggravate the threat of famine is wrong. These two must be weighed the one against the other, and what seems to be the lesser of the two must be chosen. However unsatisfactory this course of action may be, it is surely better than whitewashing an act which is of doubtful morality. The moral principles are not debased. They still stand, and this is what matters most.

It has been argued by some moralists that it can never be right deliberately to perform what is recognized by the agent to be a wrong action, and, moreover, that it can never be necessary. Although this point of view has been taken by distinguished moralists, like Bishop Sanderson, surely it is untenable. It is all very well to say that in such a dilemma the agent should take no action at all. But this will not do, for to 'take no action' may in fact lead directly to decisive consequences. We have already referred to the stock instance of the surgeon choosing between the life of the mother and the child. If he does not operate to save the life of the mother, the mother will die; whereas if he terminates the life of the infant, the mother will live. In such a case as this deliberate inaction is equivalent to action. One can be guilty[1] of the life of a drowning man just as much by failing to throw him a rope within reach as by pushing him into the river. To refrain from sterilizing a man who may beget children destined to die of starvation when the power of sterilization is in one's hand, is just as positive an action as to perform the operation. In all such cases the moral distinction between action and inaction ceases.

[1] Morally, but not legally. 'To push a man into a river so that he drowns would be a crime; to watch him drowning and to make no efforts to save him would (whatever the view of the coroner) constitute no offence in English law.' F. J. Fitzgerald: *Criminal Law and Punishment* (1962), p. 22.

CHAPTER 8

Two Contemporary Problems in Moral Theology

It will help us further to elucidate the moral and theological principles which we have been studying, if we now concentrate our attention upon what are undoubtedly two of the most urgent moral problems of the day, namely, the Problem of Sexuality, and the Problem of War. The circumstances of modern life have raised these age-long problems in new and most acute forms.

First, we take the problem of sexuality as it confronts us at the present day. Very many Christians are sorely perplexed because they hear numerous conflicting voices speaking, some of them claiming to be Christian voices. Among the latter are those which tell him that the traditional sex teaching of the Church has largely been mistaken and is out of date.

The subject falls into two parts: first, the general teaching about sex, and second, the doctrine of marriage. Beginning with general sex teaching, we proceed to consider the views of those who argue that the sex teaching of the Church in the past, going back even to New Testament times, has been in large measure erroneous and harmful, failing badly to appreciate the true nature of sex relationship. Thus, for example, Canon Sherwin Bailey has written: 'Almost from the beginning, we discern a markedly negative reaction to everything venereal which has profoundly and adversely affected the character and development of Christian sexual ideas—a reaction expressed with every degree of intensity from mild suspicion or apathy to violent hostility or revulsion. . . . The conviction rapidly gained ground and became firmly entrenched in the early Church, that coitus is not only in some indefinable sense unclean and defiling, but also intrinsically evil or sinful. . . . Closely connected with, and partly derived from, this negative view of the venereal was the sexual asceticism which has always controlled and dominated the Church's conception of sanctity, the good life, and the pursuit of perfection.'[1] Thus (it is claimed) the exaltation of virginity above marriage which characterizes the teaching not only of St. Paul but also of other New Testament writers gave the Christian doctrine of sex a dualistic twist from which it never recovered. This judgement is unsound for several reasons. In the first place, St. Paul in 1 Corinthians exalts celibacy above marriage, not because there is any dualism in his thought about sex, but because he thought that the end of the world was near. 'The time is short' (1 Cor. 7. 29). In such circumstances his attitude is fully intelligible and might well be shared by any of us if we deemed such to be the case. If we knew that an atomic war was to break out in 1966 a good many of us might perhaps hesitate before getting married—certainly before bringing children into the world.

But there was another reason behind the cult of virginity in New Testament times and that was the outbreak of State persecution. We see this reason operative in the case of the author of the Revelation of St. John which was evidently written in a time of persecution. It is clear that a married Christian would in such circumstances be in much greater danger of apostasy, fearing that, if he stood fast, not only he but his wife and family would suffer. One with no family ties would not be subjected to this terrible temptation to deny Christ. In such circumstances, surely the cult of

[1] Sherwin Bailey: *The Man-Woman Relation in Christian Thought* (1959), pp. 232–3.

virginity was fully intelligible, and we can all sympathize with it.

There is, however, a third and most important reason for saying that the attitude of the early Church towards continence was not so misguided as some would have us believe. That many of the Fathers went too far in reaction against the terrible laxity of sexual morals in the Roman Empire need not be denied; but it is only fair in passing judgement on them to bear in mind their *Sitz im Leben*. Aristotle rightly pointed out that when a stick is bent, we must bend it equally far in the opposite direction in order to straighten it. That was what the early Fathers did with sex teaching. Nor must we forget that their emphasis on strict continence both in marriage and outside it was in fact the winding up of a spring on which western culture as we understand it has depended. This point has been developed by Canon Demant in his book, *An Exposition of Christian Sex Ethics*. He writes: 'Those critics who hold that Christian sex ethics have been over-rigorous, and think that society and individuals would be better and happier with a freer sexual code, are in serious error if they believe it possible to abandon the sexual discipline and retain all the other characteristics of European civilization. The modern hedonist who considers the immediate happiness of the individual to be the sole criterion of conduct and who says he doesn't care about civilization has a strong position; but he is a sociological idiot if he believes that mankind can abandon moral effort, refuse any suppression, and relinquish every inner *ascesis* and still count on the continuance of cultural achievement. ... A disintegration of sexual morals will affect deleteriously all the other ingredients of our civilization: Its emphasis on the significance of persons, its rule of law against arbitrary power, its disinterested science, its literature and art, even its reasons for rebellion; for rebellion has to have a norm to

I

withstand. Many young people have largely lost the experience of disobedience, because nobody gives them orders except the State.'[1]

In this quotation Canon Demant uses the term 'suppression,' not as Rivers[2] who first employed it in this context to denote unwilling 'repression' in the Freudian sense, but for conscious self-control. It is unconscious or unwitting repression—an automatic process by whatever name we denote it—which is psychologically harmful. The conscious control and discipline of thoughts and desires is not hurtful but essential. Without it we should all be worse than savages.

The trouble with some of our modern Christian writers on sex is that they are far too naïve about it. We have to recognize that there is something 'daemonic' about sex. It is not a tame lap-dog but a lion, magnificent but dangerous. This characteristic of sex is the basis of the ancient idea that sex is 'unclean.' This point is widely misunderstood by modern writers—even by writers who ought to know better. To the ancient Hebrew the idea of uncleanness was equated with the 'numinous' and the supernatural 'daemonic.'[3] In modern modes of thought the unclean and the common tend to be associated; not so in the ancient world where the unclean stood with the holy. Thus Ezekiel wrote of his ideal community: 'They shall teach my people the difference between the holy and the profane, and cause them to discern between the unclean and the clean' (*Ezek.* 44. 23). Here holy and unclean are parallel on the one side, and profane and clean on the other. Thus the mysteries of both birth— menstruation—and death—a corpse—were 'unclean' because they take us beyond the confines of this mortal life. Therefore in like manner everything directly associated with sex

---

[1] V. A. Demant: *op. cit.*, pp. 94 and 95.
[2] W. H. R. Rivers: *Instinct and the Unconscious* (1920), p. 17.
[3] See R. Otto: *The Idea of the Holy, passim.*

is unclean because it is ultimately mysterious and holy—not because there is something evil and wicked about it. That idea is entirely foreign to the Old Testament, where, as the Rabbis frequently pointed out, the first commandment in the Scriptures is: 'Be fruitful and multiply' (*Gen.* 1. 22). There is nothing dualistic here; the same applies to the New Testament. Those modern writers, therefore, who reproach the Church for having thought of sexual intercourse in terms of dualistic teaching because it has been regarded as 'unclean' have failed entirely to understand the Old Testament idiom. At its best, sex is the noblest of all our instinctive drives; but it is sheer self-deception to suppose that it is not also the most dangerous. If it is allowed to get out of hand it can turn civilization into a cess-pool. That is what happened in the Graeco-Roman world; and it is only against that background that the traditional sex teaching of the Church can be properly understood. What is more, the evidence of the present day relating to these matters suggests that we are not entirely free from the danger of relapsing into a similar condition. The age in which one of our popular entertainments is a striptease is obviously heading in this direction. This is not due to sexual starvation as some would suggest. On all sides we see sex flaunted before us. We are not sex-obsessed because of our inherited Victorianism. That is as dead as the Middle Ages. We are sex-obsessed largely because this part of our nature has for the past generation been over-stimulated, mainly by those who are actuated by commercial motives. The way to deal with the present situation, therefore, is to recognize that in the case of sex we are dealing with something which is highly inflammable, instead of continually nagging Mother Church for her lack of understanding and sympathy in this matter in the past. There has been a good deal more wisdom in her attitude—even if she has sometimes erred—than some modern Christian writers seem to realize.

I said a few moments ago that we are sex-obsessed to-day because of sex propaganda and wicked exploitation of sex for commercial reasons; but this is not the whole story. Those who are responsible for this racket would have no power at all if there were not some deep underlying cause which leads men and women to turn to sex so easily when they are outwardly frustrated. Dr. Demant is surely right when he says of the modern situation that it is 'marked by an obsession with sex for non-sexual reasons.' And he goes on to point out that 'the resort to indiscriminate sexual experience does not appear to be a great source of joy and freedom.'[1]

The modern world is a frustrated world, harassed by a sense of insecurity on a vast scale. In the experience of sex we have recourse to something elemental which brings a temporary sense of release and self-expression. In this the experience is analogous to that which comes from drink. The drunkard who told the magistrate that he did this because it was 'the quickest way out of Salford,' where he lived in a slum, was voicing the meaning of this very clearly. It is not sexuality which is ultimately to blame, any more than alcohol is ultimately to blame. The fault lies in a world in which men's values are topsy turvy and in which they suffer continual frustration, especially frustration of the higher impulses of personality. But this need not cause us to think that the Church has been to blame in warning men against the fallacy of supposing that we can safely indulge our sexual propensities without restriction. The evidence, on the contrary, does nothing but corroborate the belief that the traditional teaching of the Church in this matter has been right.

Another way in which the traditional sex teaching of the Church has been called to account is in respect of her teaching about the place of women in society, and the upholding of the patriarchal tradition, according to which,

[1] *Op. cit.*, p. 111.

we are told, women have been downtrodden and subjected to something not far removed from slavery. St. Paul is the great enemy here and has been accused of gross subordinationism in his regulations concerning women and their place in Christian worship.

In this attack on tradition there are several strands which, in the interests of clear thinking, must be disentangled. In the first place, it should be clearly understood that it is Christian teaching and Christian teaching alone which has stood for the equality of the sexes. As Lecky, who was no Christian apologist, pointed out, the establishing of strict monogamy by the Church did more to secure for woman her place as the equal of man than anything else.[1] Nor is this equality inconsistent with the acceptance of the patriarchal tradition. It is very easy to think of the latter as it existed in the Old Testament, beginning with polygamy and progressing to monogamy of a kind in which man is the boss and his wife one of his chattels, along with his house, and his servants, and his cattle, as stated in the Tenth Commandment. But Christian monogamy changed all that, although it has taken many centuries to win its way. The Church has held fast to St. Paul's dictum that in Christ all divisions of race, economic status and sexual discrimination are transcended.[2]

Nor is what he says elsewhere about women really inconsistent with this. When we recall that by upbringing he was 'an Hebrew of the Hebrews,' as he himself says, this is the more remarkable. Professor Anderson Scott[3] has pointed out that, whereas it is true that the Apostle speaks of the husband being the head of the wife (1 Cor. 11. 3) he also speaks of God being the head of Christ in the same breath. Since he is at pains to show elsewhere that our Lord was on

[1] W. E. H. Lecky: *History of European Morals* (1913), II. 282.
[2] Galatians 3. 28.
[3] C. Anderson Scott, *New Testament Ethics* (1942), p. 126.

an equality with God (*Phil.* 2. 3) it is clear that, for him, headship cannot be reconciled with the idea of subordination. Again, when in Ephesians 5. 22 ff. St. Paul (or the Pauline writer) calls upon wives to 'submit'[1] themselves to their husbands, it must be carefully observed that this is exactly what in the previous verse is required of all Christians in their relation to one another. It is a *mutual* relationship. 'Submit,' therefore, is surely not the best rendering. Anderson Scott suggests 'defer' and this brings out the meaning.

As for the patriarchal tradition, what are we going to put in its place? Historically it has undoubtedly been the most beneficial of all. Canon Demant, writing as a student of sociology, says truly: 'Because of the security and assurance which the child of a monogamous and patriarchal family enjoys, the young of the European family have shown an enterprise and constructive social power not reached elsewhere. Of course, the patriarchal family requires of its members a good deal of renunciation. The wife must be chaste and devoted to the family, the children must be taught to obey and to endure discipline; the husband takes on much personal responsibility beyond merely providing for the physical needs of the household. The family under these conditions has added many functions to its basic sexual and reproductive ones. That is why the patriarchal family pattern has been such a great force in the development of social culture.'[2]

This brings us to a question much canvassed at the present time, and that is the legitimacy of extra-marital sexual intercourse, or fornication. In the Christian tradition from the first this has been condemned without qualification, but to-day there are responsible voices pressing the question, Is it *per se* wrong, or may it be lawful in certain circumstances?

---

[1] It is perhaps significant that the actual word ὑποτάσσεσθε is omitted in the best text.
[2] *Op. cit.*, p. 104.

An affirmative answer to the latter question was given by Professor Carstairs recently, his argument being that, provided that contraceptive devices are used to prevent the birth of offspring, it is good that the young should have some practice in the art of sexual intercourse before having to settle down to the real thing in marriage. He said: 'Biologically children are capable of enjoying sexual relationships from the age of puberty. In many societies they are positively encouraged to do so; every young Trobriand Island boy and girl, every young Samoan, every young member of Indian jungle tribes like the Maria has had many sexual experiences before their betrothal and wedding. The interesting thing is that this pre-marital licence has been found to be quite compatible with stable married life.'[1] Professor Carstairs then goes on rather inconsequently to ask: 'Is chastity the supreme moral virtue?' as if Christians had ever asserted that it was. The relevant question is whether chastity is a virtue at all, not whether or not it is the supreme virtue.

Professor Carstairs thinks that it is not, and he bases his position on two grounds. The first, already mentioned, is that extra-marital intercourse is quite consistent with a settled married life as is shown by the empirical evidence drawn from various primitive peoples. The second reason which he gives is that pre-marital sexual experience, with due precautions against conception, 'makes it *more likely* that marriage, when it comes, will be a mutually considerate and mutually satisfying partnership'[2] (italics ours). This is a large claim, but he cites no evidence whatever to support it. It would indeed be extremely difficult to secure such evidence, but at least he should have discussed the question of this evidence carefully. As it stands, the statement is empirically valueless, and the position which Professor Carstairs advocates is left without any solid support. It

[1] G. M. Carstairs: *This Island Now* (1963), p. 50.   [2] *Ibid.*, p. 51.

would certainly be possible to obtain evidence to show that pre-marital sexual intercourse has a most adverse effect upon subsequent marriage relations. The only conclusion which is possible at present is to say that this attempt to bolster up extra-marital intercourse must be written off.

Nevertheless, those who advocate the legitimacy of extra-marital intercourse are entitled to ask those who condemn it to give their reasons; and this can and should be done. For those who accept the authority of the New Testament, there is, of course, no room for doubt. Fornication is condemned there as *per se* sinful; but we are not left with an unreasoned condemnation. It is condemned on the ground that sexual intercourse brings the two parties together in such a degree of intimacy that in some mysterious sense they become one, in such wise that they can never be the same again. So St. Paul wrote: 'Know ye not that he that is joined to a harlot is one body? for, the twain, saith he, shall become one flesh.'[1] To this the Apostle adds a further argument to the effect that the body of the Christian is the shrine of the indwelling Spirit, so that he must keep it holy and is not free to do as he likes with it. But, of course, this second argument depends upon the validity of the former, and is a kind of rider to it. This position can be defended by an appeal to empirical evidence. On this ground it can be maintained that this intimate relationship implies in its nature such a deep involvement that when it is lightly or casually or purely experimentally performed it has harmful effects on the personality and fosters irresponsibility and self-gratification. The evidence certainly suggests that it is only when it is accompanied by deep care and respect in addition to strong physical attraction that it is really satisfying, and this means when it is performed within the context of marriage. Even the Trobriand Islanders cut out fornication in the form of adultery and thus implicitly recognize

[1] 1 Corinthians 6. 16.

this. 'Any . . . breach of marital fidelity is as severely condemned in the Trobriands as it is in Christian principle.'[1]

There is, however, another consideration which has to be taken into account. We have seen that Professor Carstairs recognizes that extra-marital intercourse is permissible only when precautions are taken to prevent conception. If a child results from the act, it is admitted that the whole position is changed. There are, however, many Christians who hold that, despite all that has been said, to use contraceptive devices is an unnatural act, and therefore wrong. In some circumstances, they would say, to use these devices may be legitimate as the lesser of two evils. But it would hardly be argued that fornication provides such circumstances. It follows, therefore, that if the use of contraceptive devices is wrong, extra-marital intercourse in all circumstances is wrong. On the other hand, even if the use of contraceptives within marriage is to be admitted, it certainly does not follow that it is legitimate to use them outside it.

The upshot of this discussion must be that, to say the very least, empirically the evidence is indecisive. Those who agree with Professor Carstairs will go on saying that the evidence shows that sexual experimentation of this kind before marriage is harmless and even positively beneficial provided that conception is ruled out. Others will argue that the empirical evidence shows that sexual intercourse involves the parties to it so deeply that, unless it is confined to marriage, it is damaging to their personalities, and bound to be so. Once again, it is impossible to reach the empirical evidence in such a way as to be conclusive. Ultimately we are driven back to the authority of the Holy Spirit in the New Testament, which unequivocally condemns it and declares chastity to be a virtue. But there is no evidence that it is held to be the chief virtue; yet this does not rule it out any more than it excludes the fact that faith and hope

[1] B. Malinowski: *The Sexual Life of Savages* (1948), p. 98.

are also virtues, even if 'the greatest of these is charity.'
Nor is it at all easy to see that because charity is the queen
of the virtues, according to Christian teaching, that does
anything at all to underwrite the legitimacy of sexual intercourse outside marriage. Here is a sheer *non sequitur*.

We now come to the problem of sex in relation to
marriage. Marriage is a natural institution. Although it
may take different forms: polygamy, polygyny, monogamy
and so forth, it is a natural and not a man-made institution.
The first members of the human race did not get together
and say: 'Go to, now, we will have marriage instead of
promiscuity.' They found it natural to have stable sexual
relations.

When our Lord came into the world and began to teach,
he was questioned by his disciples about the nature of
marriage and especially about divorce. He did not refuse on
this occasion, as was sometimes the case, to give a direct
answer to their questions. His answer was clear and unambiguous even if it was in some quarters unacceptable.
He said that although Moses allowed divorce, he was
mistaken. In the mind of the Creator there was no such
thought. Man and wife should respectively leave their
parents and 'stick together' and nobody should separate
them.

This teaching was taken up by St. Paul (or the Paulinist)
in the Epistle to the Ephesians,[1] where the union between
man and wife was likened to the union between Christ and
his church, called by the writer a mystery—in Latin,
Sacramentum. It was impossible to put the matter more
strongly, and this, from the first, has been the tradition of
the Church.

As time went on, and the influence of Roman law made
itself felt in Christianity, the doctrine of marriage as a
contract, found in Roman law, as it had previously existed

[1] Ephesians 5. 32.

in Hebrew thought, was made part and parcel of the Christian doctrine of marriage. That is to say, the marriage is complete once the contract has been made—complete in the sense of being a true marriage, without waiting for the consummation and the birth of children. This accorded well with the belief that Adam and Eve were truly man and wife as also were Joseph and Mary, although there was no question of consummation. But it was a contract of a special kind. It was a contract that conferred a status.

Thus, according to Christian teaching, marriage exists in two forms: (*a*) Natural Marriage, common to all members of the human race: (*b*) Christian or sacramental marriage, when the contracting parties are baptized Christians. But in respect of permanence and indissolubility there is no difference between them. Otherwise Christian marriage could not be truly a sacrament. For the Christian sacraments require what is natural as a basis. In Baptism it is water, in the Holy Eucharist it is bread and wine, which is taken up into the supernatural plane. Even so, in Christian marriage, the blessing of God comes upon the contracting parties, who are the ministers of the sacrament in this case, and the natural institution becomes a sacrament. Thus there is no truth at all in the common belief that marriage in a Register Office is less permanent in its nature than marriage in church. Both are permanent, but Christian marriage confers special grace on the parties in response to prayer to fulfil their vows. Hence in the Prayer Book it is said to be 'a remedy against sin,' which is a technical term for a sacrament. All the Church's sacraments are remedies against sin. If there were no sin, there would be no need of sacraments.

What, then, is the purpose of the institution of marriage? According to the Book of Common Prayer there are said to be three such purposes: (i) the building up and care of the family; (ii) a means of grace to live together; (iii) mutual society and fellowship. 'It is not good for man to be alone.'

In some quarters at the present day this teaching is being questioned—particularly in respect of the first reason given. Not only is it denied that it is the primary purpose of marriage. In some quarters it is denied that it is an essential purpose at all. This has brought great confusion in the minds of many as to what marriage is all about. We are now being told that the real purpose of marriage is the establishing of the 'mutual society, help and comfort' by means of sexual intercourse which brings about 'one flesh.' This has been made entirely possible without any real danger of childbearing by the perfecting of contraceptive devices. Thus children, we are taught, are only an appendix to marriage—a delightful appendix some will say—but, nevertheless, not of its essence. One modern Christian writer has performed the *tour de force* of writing a long book on sex and marriage without once mentioning the subject of parenthood!

Those who sponsor this novel doctrine of marriage claim to be guided by empirical evidence. They assert that marriages which are carried out on this basis are happier and healthier than those of the past when fear of unwanted children haunted the sexual life of the man as well as the woman. The traditional doctrine that there is a given pattern in nature to which coitus should conform is therefore untrue. It is as natural (or more natural) to conduct coital relations with contraceptives as without them. What is called 'the relational' aspect of sex is as fundamental and important as the generative. Man and wife become 'one flesh' in this way, and that (we are told) is the primary purpose of marriage. It is argued, moreover, that since nature is infertile during the woman's 'safe' period, there can be nothing unnatural in extending this safety period artificially.

It is important at this point to distinguish carefully between two positions which are frequently confused. We must distinguish between those who still hold to the traditional doctrine of marriage as set forth in the Prayer Book but who also hold that, in certain circumstances, the use of contraceptives is permissible, and, on the other hand, those who positively glory in contraceptives and believe that they have enabled mankind for the first time in human history to appreciate the true nature of marriage as the establishing of the 'One Flesh' union apart altogether from the generative function of sex. It is the rise of this second type of doctrine, in the name of Christianity, which poses for the present-day moral theologian the chief problem. 'Thus a justification for contraception is found, not in any special circumstances, but in the nature of the marriage relationship itself.'[1]

The moral theologian, faced by a revolution like this in respect of the doctrine of marriage, will of necessity proceed with the utmost caution. On any showing, the institution of marriage is of such vital importance that we cannot afford to take any chances. The apostles of this new teaching, indeed, advance their opinions with the utmost confidence, but 'it is, to say the least, suspicious that the age in which contraception has won its way is not one which has been conspicuously successful in managing its sexual life. Is it possible that, by claiming the right to manipulate his physical processes in this matter, man may, without knowing or intending it, be stepping over the boundary between the world of Christian marriage and what one might call the world of Aphrodite—the world of sterile eroticism against which the Church reacted so strongly (perhaps too strongly) in its early days?'[2]

It may well be true, as the authors of *The Family in Contemporary Society* say, that the early Fathers reacted too strongly against the sexual thought and practice of their days; but it does not follow that we are right in abandoning the principles of marriage they held because they pressed

---

[1] *The Family in Contemporary Society*, p. 130.   [2] *Ibid.*, p. 135.

them too far. However we may look at man's sexual nature, one thing is clear: it easily gets out of hand. There is an element of *inordinatio* or *concupiscentia* in it which we ignore at our own peril. But this is something of which the authors of what we may perhaps call the Novel Doctrine of Marriage seem to be totally unaware.

How, then, is the moral theologian to understand the problem of marriage? Is he justified in saying that the primary purpose of marriage is the building up of the family in the light of empirical evidence alleged to show the elevating and liberating effects of modern contraceptives? Or should he still hold fast, as his guiding principle, the traditional belief that generation (which, from the biological view, is obviously the primary purpose of marriage) is to be understood as such from the spiritual and psychological points of view also? It is hard to deny this. The marriage relationship clearly finds its fulfilment in 'the gift and heritage of children'; and it is to fly in the face of facts to ignore this. The modern 'two stage' marriage, rendered possible by modern contraception, is wrong in principle. If a couple cannot afford 'to start a family' as soon as they marry, they should wait until they can afford it. The marriage union of Christians is a complete mutual dedication of man and wife for the establishing (if God wills) of a Christian family. This is the presupposition which underlies the whole of the marriage service in the Book of Common Prayer, where prayer is offered that the parties 'may both be fruitful in the procreation of children,' and not that they may successfully establish the 'one flesh' relationship.

It should here be pointed out, furthermore, that the Novel Doctrine of Marriage does not underwrite its permanent nature, let alone its indissolubility, as does the traditional doctrine. Advocates of the Novel Doctrine admit openly that the one-flesh relationship may break down in such a way as to be beyond repair. In such cases the marriage should be regarded as at an end and the parties should be free to enter into another marital relationship. According to the traditional doctrine, however, in which marriage is rooted in the family, it is the existence of the children which requires a strict and lasting monogamy. The biological and psychological evidence is decisive here. The young of the human species are dependent upon their parents for a long period of years which has no parallel in any other animal species. This means that by the time the children are all independent the wife has normally passed the age of child-bearing. Hence marriage is 'in its nature a union permanent and life-long.'[1] According to the Novel Doctrine it is not permanent *in its nature*.

At this point we must take note of an argument which is often adduced to support the Novel Doctrine, but which in fact is quite irrelevant. It is to the effect that since 'natural' coitus may be immorally performed—e.g. to gratify lust —'the allegedly "natural" performance of the act cannot *per se* guarantee the benefits attributed to it.'[2] Of course this is true. Any natural act can be immorally performed. Eating, for example, may be immoral, if it is done from a gluttonous motive; but this does not alter the fact that it is a natural act, recognized by everybody to be the normal way of introducing nourishment into the healthy human body rather than the method of intravenous injection, which, in that case, would be unnatural. Likewise there is a natural pattern of sexual intercourse which carries with it the possibility of procreation of children, which cannot be brought about normally in any other way. If we reject that pattern— which includes not only the procreation but also the nurture of children—and substitute another one for it, we are endangering the whole institution of marriage in the

[1] See Draft Canon B. 29 in the proposed revised Canons of the Church of England.
[2] *The Family in Contemporary Society*, p. 147.

interests of an empiricism, the results of which are still far
from clear. It does not follow from this, of course, that the
use of contraceptives is never permissible. Their use may
well be in many cases the lesser of two evils. But this is an
entirely different matter from saying that their use is essential
for the satisfactory fulfilment of marriage. The empiricists
will have to produce a great deal more evidence than has
so far appeared before they can begin to establish such a
thesis.

There are, indeed, formidable difficulties in their way. In
the first place, there is the extraordinary difficulty of obtaining the required evidence. Thus we are told by advocates
of the Novel Doctrine of Marriage 'that contraception
appears to promote the highest ends of sexual union.'[1] The
word 'appears' in this statement suggests that the empirical
evidence is vague. Again, what are 'the highest ends of
sexual union'? We are not told. Clearly they must be
estimated according to the doctrine of marriage which is
presupposed, and our empiricism fails us for it involves us
in a vicious circle. The highest ends must be judged by our
doctrine of marriage, but our doctrine of marriage (we are
told) can be determined only by the empirical evidence.
Yet again, does the habitual use of contraceptives undermine
the power of self-control in marriage? The question is
plainly one of great importance, but it is quite impossible
to obtain empirical evidence necessary to provide a clear
answer to it. Still yet again, are the psychological and non-
biological effects of intercourse during the 'safe period' the
same as those of coitus during artificial sterility, or not? So
far as I know, there is no evidence at all to enable us to
answer this question, and it is difficult to see how there
could be.

In the end, we are brought to the point when it becomes
clear that it is really impossible to establish any doctrine of

[1] *Op. cit.*, p. 147.

marriage empirically. We are driven back on moral judgements which must be based on other grounds. This applies
just as much to the upholders of the Novel Doctrine of
Marriage as to the upholders of the traditional doctrine.
Surely the burden of proof must lie on those who challenge
the traditional doctrine which has commended itself to the
mind of the Church for many centuries? So far the proof
is not in sight. That is the only conclusion which a sound
moral theology can reach.

There is another way in which the doctrine and practice
of marriage have been fundamentally challenged by modern
thought and methods, and that is by the development of the
technique of artificial human insemination. This has raised
grave moral questions to which we must now give our close
attention. Artificial insemination has for many years
been employed in cattle breeding but artificial insemination
among human beings is a modern invention. It exists in
two forms. The first, often called homologous, is when
the semen of the husband is used (A.I.H.). The second, or
heterologous, procedure is when the semen is obtained from
another man (A.I.D.). Sometimes, a mixture of the two is
employed, but in this case the practice falls really under the
second category. The former is used when there is impo-
tence, vaginal spasm, painful coitus (dyspareunia), sterility,
failure to ejaculate, and in one or two other circumstances.
The latter is used mainly when there is male sterility, or
hereditary disease or defect in the husband. It may also be
used when it is desired to have the paternity of a man en-
dowed with outstanding qualities. It is difficult to say how
widespread the practice is in either form. Very different
estimates have been made. It seems to be clear, however,
that in both forms it is on the increase, and it is, therefore,
of the highest importance to assess its moral and social
significance. The moral theologian, of course, is concerned
only with its ethical aspect, and not primarily with its legal

K

or social significance. Thus we shall not attempt to discuss the question as to whether A.I.D. should be made a crime.

Turning first to A.I.H., it is clear at once that it does not raise the same problems for the Christian as does A.I.D. On the assumption that the procreation and nurture of children is the primary purpose of marriage, it might seem at first sight to raise no moral problem at all. This, however, is unfortunately not the case; for the question as to how the semen is obtained cannot be avoided. It may be obtained as a result of sexual intercourse between the spouses, the semen subsequently being conveyed by instruments into the vagina. This is commonly known as 'assisted insemination' and this is generally approved by Christian moral theology, inasmuch as it is not more than an extension of the normal act of intercourse, removing its defects, even as a pair of spectacles removes the defects of eyesight. This has received the imprimatur of the Pope himself, who in condemning other forms of A.I.H. expressly excluded 'the use of certain artificial means designed only to facilitate the natural act or to enable that act, performed in a natural manner, to attain its end.'[1] If, however, the semen is obtained apart from the natural act of intercourse (e.g. by masturbation or *coitus interruptus*) it is condemned by the Roman Catholic Church on the ground that these are sinful practices and that the end does not justify the means. Prior to the Papal pronouncement some Roman Catholic moralists sought to justify it by means of the principle of double effect, whereby it is asserted that when a single action has two effects, one good and one bad, it is justified by the former. This must be distinguished from the maxim that the end justifies the means. It is not a question of two actions, one bad leading to one good, but a single act with two consequences. It is, however, hard to see how, for example, masturbation in such circumstances could really be regarded

[1] Address to Second World Congress on Fertility and Sterility, 19th May, 1956.

as other than a separate act from the act of intercourse; and there are probably no moral theologians who would seek to defend the practice to-day in this way. Nevertheless, there are outside the Roman Church not a few moralists who would defend A.I.H. by means of masturbation or by *coitus interruptus* or other means in cases of necessity. They would argue that (for example) masturbation *in that context* ceased to be an act of self-indulgence by being brought into the context of sexual intercourse, and therefore is not *per se* wrong. The findings of the Archbishop's Commission in 1948 probably represent the point of view of most Christian moralists outside the Roman Church in this matter. They say: 'All but one of the members of the Commission were agreed that: When "assisted insemination" is inapplicable, or ineffective, other methods of artificial insemination with the husband's semen may be employed. Even if, for the insemination of a wife with her husband's semen, there is no practicable alternative to masturbation by the husband, his act, being directed to the procreative end of the marriage, may be justifiable.'[1]

Thus far A.I.H. We now turn to the far more difficult question of A.I.D. which raises a formidable number of moral questions, in addition to the legal questions, with which we are not now *directly* concerned.

The first question which arises is whether A.I.D. constitutes adultery. Here the moral theologian must note that the lawyers are divided. As far back as 1921 in the now celebrated case of Orford *v.* Orford in Canada in which a wife sued her husband for alimony, explaining the existence of a child, of which he was admittedly not the father, by asserting that she had submitted herself to A.I.D. The plea was disallowed on the ground that she had committed adultery. The judge, commenting on the case, said that the essence of adultery does not consist in sexual intercourse but

---

[1] *Artificial Human Insemination* (S.P.C.K. 1948), p. 58.

in the voluntary surrender of reproductive powers to a third party. On the other hand, in the case of Maclennan *v.* Maclennan in 1958, the judge (Lord Wheatley) argued that the sole test of adultery is sexual intercourse, and not impregnation. A similar opinion underlies the English case of Baxter *v.* Baxter where it was decided that the use of contraceptives was not a bar to consummation.

Those theologians who defend A.I.D. against the charge of adultery, have adopted a different ground from the lawyers. Thus the present Dean of St. Paul's in his minority Report to that of the Archbishop's Commission maintained that 'only on a crassly materialistic hypothesis of the meaning of the words can A.I.D., when carried out at the request of the husband and with due precautions against injustice to others, be called adulterous. The spiritual elements which constitute the sin of adultery are absent. I have been interested to notice that all the lay people to whom I have mentioned the fact that some theologians regard A.I.D., as defined above, as equivalent to adultery received the information with incredulity. The law of love is often thought to be too vague to form the basis for moral judgements. This, however, is not so. The principle of love requires that we shall seek the good of all beings who may be affected by our conduct.'[1] Again, Mr. Joseph Fletcher argues that marriage is not so much a legal or material relationship as one which is personal and spiritual, and that A.I.D. does no violence to marriage thus understood.[2] In both these judgements we see the depreciation of the material in the supposed interests of the spiritual. This, however, is to advocate a very dubious theology from the Christian point of view. In the often quoted remark of Archbishop William Temple, Christianity is the most materialistic of all the great religions, and its doctrine of

---

[1] *Ibid.*, pp. 61 and 62.   [2] J. Fletcher: *Morals and Medicine* (1955), p. 139.

marriage clearly indicates that. Marriage is, beyond question, rooted in human flesh: in the flesh of husband and wife and in the production of the flesh of the children. It is not a union of pure spirits. It is not possible to estimate its significance without holding fast all the time to the material basis. The family *per se* has a material basis. Adultery is primarily wrong not because it undermines the mutual trust of husband and wife—many other deeds can equally do that—but because it jeopardizes the material basis of the family and casts doubt upon the paternity of the offspring. It is, therefore, to go much too far to assert, as does the Dean of St. Paul's, that in A.I.D. 'the spiritual elements which constitute the sin of adultery are absent.' Ultimately the desire to have children regardless of their paternity may be just as selfish as the desire which leads to a conventional act of adultery. The question which has to be faced is whether the risk to the stability of the institution of marriage which A.I.D. undeniably involves is (to use the words of Dean Matthews) for 'the good of all beings.' He would be a bold man who would confidently assert that it is. It is at least arguable that A.I.D. presents a more dangerous threat to marriage as an institution than does adultery, inasmuch as it can be made to appear morally respectable, whereas, even to-day, the latter still carries a stigma with it.

Those who defend A.I.D. usually make a strong point of the existence of the husband's consent, implying that, apart from that, it is morally quite indefensible. This assumption, however, needs to be carefully examined. It is more than questionable. The authors of the chapter entitled 'The Legal Aspects of Artificial Insemination' in the Report of the Archbishop's Committee rightly say: 'We find a strange inconsistency in the principle that married couples desirous of ostensible issue should be permitted by the law to achieve their object by the insemination of the wife *aliunde* but not permitted to do so by the concealed introduction of a child begotten by the husband born of a woman other than the wife, whether normally or by means of his service as donor. We cannot think that the advocates of A.I.D. would consider the latter expedient to be justified. To our minds it is no better and no worse than the other.'[1] The pertinent question here is: If the consent of the husband validates the former procedure, why should not the consent of the wife validate the latter? If the latter is held to be a sinful infringement of the marriage relationship, by what process of reasoning can the former be upheld? In other words, it seems to follow that any husband who gives permission to his wife to submit to A.I.D. is acting *ultra vires*. Surely the fundamental mistake which is made by the advocates of A.I.D. is that they are too much inclined to think of marriage as being a private contract between husband and wife, so that, provided all is 'above board' between them, no infringement of the contract is made. Marriage, however, as understood by Christians, is more than a contract; it is an 'estate' or institution, ordained by God, and under the dominion of God alone.

From the point of view of the moral theologian, however, the question, whether or not A.I.D. is to be equated with adultery is not the primary question which it is for the lawyer. The primary question is whether it is right or wrong *per se*; and this, in turn, seems to depend upon two considerations, over and above those which have already been examined. The first is how far A.I.D. necessitates absolute secrecy, or, to use plain language, fraud. It is generally maintained by the advocates of A.I.D. that absolute secrecy is essential. 'Presumably it has a threefold basis. It protects the spouses from harmful comment and gossip, safeguards the donor's reputation and frees him from risk of blackmail, and protects the psychological security of the

---

[1] *Op. cit.*, p. 41.

child.'[1] If this secrecy is strictly observed, the whole procedure is an act of fraud; and this alone is sufficient to bring
it under the condemnation of the Christian moralist. Herein
it differs entirely from the procedure of adoption, which is
public, and in which (if the wise course is followed) the
children concerned are not kept in the dark. It is, indeed,
possible that A.I.D. births might be subject to compulsory
registration with a number in place of the donor's name.
Unless, however, the child concerned is to be allowed to
know the situation (so far as the mother knows it) the charge
of fraud still stands. If, on the other hand, the child is to be
told that he is a 'test-tube baby,' the psychological risk is so
great that the majority of A.I.D. advocates would not
contemplate this possibility.

Apart from the question of fraud, there is another vital
consideration which the moral theologian must take into
consideration in seeking to assess A.I.D., and that is the
threat which it presents to the institution of the family. The
essential structure of the family is based on the community
of parents and their natural offspring. A.I.D. introduces an
alien factor. It is not scaremongering to assert that the
practice might well develop to such dimensions as to undermine fatally the security of the family by the wholesale
introduction unawares of half-brothers and half-sisters into
its structure, which would inevitably lead to incestuous
marriages. Not many moral theologians will be impressed
by Mr. Fletcher's arguments drawn from alleged Old
Testament parallels in the family-community conception of
the parental relationship,[2] for the simple reason that Christianity is based, according to our Lord's teaching, upon a
monogamous and not a polygamous view of marriage. In
any case, there is no parallel to A.I.D. here, since at least
everything was above board in those far-off days.

[1] N. St. John Stevas: *Life, Death and the Law*, p. 143.　[2] *Op. cit.*, p. 119.

In the course of this book we have again and again asked ourselves the question, how far it is legitimate to base our moral theology upon conceptions of natural law and the alleged constitution of human nature, and how far we should base our morals upon more empirical factors. We must, therefore, face the question how far the latter may lead us to modify the conclusions to which we have been led in condemnation of A.I.D. Once again, we are faced by the old difficulty of obtaining reliable evidence. In the very nature of A.I.D. this is inevitable, because of the veil of secrecy in which it is shrouded. What is really required is to have access to the case histories of a large number of A.I.D. children; but this seems to be crying for the moon. The empirical evidence, such as it is, is extremely scanty, as well as being limited in scope. For what has to be taken into account is not merely the happiness or otherwise of A.I.D. families but the effect of the practice of A.I.D. upon marriage and society at large. Looking, however, at the immediate field of the A.I.D. family itself the evidence is not only scanty but indecisive. The benefit to the wife is by no means to be taken for granted. Her desire for maternity which makes her ready to seek and accept the seed of a man who is not her husband may well 'be judged to be pathological.'[1] Accordingly it may constitute a psychological blunder to pander to it. The benefit to the child born and nurtured on a fraudulent basis is still more doubtful. Moreover, the number of cases concerning which it is possible to assess the empirical evidence is still very small, and, furthermore, the majority of A.I.D. children are too young at present to afford reliable evidence. Moreover, the doctors who have engaged in this practice and who have also recorded their views as to its merits do not speak with one

[1] *Artificial Human Insemination*, p. 25.

voice.[1] Clearly the empirical evidence so far is too slight, even in the limited field of the families immediately concerned, to make it possible to form a balanced judgement on that basis.

The crucial question here is plainly whether it is legitimate to take the undeniably great risks involved in A.I.D. in order, if possible, to gain adequate empirical evidence by which to judge it. Judging by the morality of inspiration, the answer must be negative. Not only in Catholic Christendom, but far beyond it, there is moral objection to A.I.D. which goes much deeper than mere aesthetic repugnance to the act. This opposition is based on the belief that here is something which *per se* violates the integrity of marriage as the *consortium totius vitae* of one man and one woman to the exclusion of all others. The mind of Christendom must be judged to be against the adoption of the experimental approach here.

Let us now turn to another major moral problem which faces the world to-day, and that is the problem of war. It is unfortunately no new problem *per se*, but it has now presented itself in an entirely new form so that in the eyes of many the traditional treatment of this question is obsolete and useless. Nevertheless, it will be well for us first to consider in outline what the traditional teaching in this matter is.

A convenient starting point is the statement in the 37th of the Thirty-nine Articles, in the Latin version. It is as follows: *Christianis licet et ex mandato magistratus arma portare et justa bella administrare.* There are three points here which must be noticed. First, it is said that it is *lawful* for Christians to engage in war. It is not said that all Christians are morally bound to fight when called upon to do so. The individual Christian may have scruples, and, if so, it is implied that the

---

[1] See N. St. John Stevas, *op. cit.*, pp. 153, 154 for a brief summary of the medical evidence.

state should respect those scruples. A place is allowed for 'the conscientious objector,' and this has been implemented by the government of this country in the past. Secondly, a Christian can be required to fight only 'at the command of the magistrate,' i.e. by the duly constituted authority of the state. This is an important consideration as we shall see in a moment. Thirdly, it is only *justa bella* in which the Christian is justified in taking part. Here the Latin version is much more accurate than the English version of the article, which merely says that it is lawful for the Christian 'to serve in the wars.'

On what ground is this statement, which is in strict accord with the age-long tradition of the Church, based? In the main, on two grounds. In the first place, it is nowhere definitely stated in the New Testament that it is sinful for a Christian to be a soldier. On the contrary, as Aquinas points out, following Augustine, the advice given by John the Baptist to the soldiers implies the reverse. He did not say to them: Throw away your arms, but: Do violence to no man and be content with your wages.[1] In the second place, it is based upon the New Testament teaching that the state is the ordinance of God and that the magistrate 'beareth not the sword in vain' (*Rom.* 13. 4; cf. 1 *Peter* 2. 13). The state, however, depends upon justice and this involves the use of force against its enemies, whether internal or external. In other words, law requires for its maintenance the use of sanctions. Nor is this affected by the saying of our Lord, 'Resist not evil,' which is not relevant to this situation. As Grotius said, in his great work *De Jure Belli et Pacis*: 'Christ is not here addressing magistrates.' He is talking about personal relationships, which, he taught, must be governed by 'love' (*agape*). The relation of states, however, cannot be directed in this way. It must be governed by justice. It is simply meaningless to say that states must love one another;

[1] S.T. 2a. 2ae. Q. 40. a. 1.

for love is a personal relationship and states are not persons. Nor, according to the tradition of the Church, is it relevant to quote the sixth commandment; for this is rightly translated to mean 'Thou shalt do no murder,' not, 'Thou shalt not kill,' both in its original form in Exodus 20. 17 and in its Deuteronomic form (Deut. 5. 17). The ordinary Hebrew word for killing (harag) is avoided and the word regularly used for murder (ratsah) is employed. In the third place, this traditional teaching is based upon the conception of the 'just war,' and it is here that, in the opinion of many, it breaks down in modern circumstances. We must, therefore, submit it to most careful consideration.

The conditions of a just war are defined by Aquinas, who states the traditional view very clearly, as being three. First, the war must be declared by the lawful authority of the state. Private wars are ruled out. We have already noted the reason for this, which is that the state is based upon justice and justice in the last resort depends upon force. Secondly, the war must have a just cause, viz. self-defence or the redressing of injuries. Thirdly, it must have a right intention and this must be the promotion of good and the avoiding of evil.[1] Ultimately, this means, as Aquinas says, that only those wars are just whose objective is peace. This means that if a war is to be a just war it must have a strictly limited objective. The objective of 'unconditional surrender,' which was unfortunately proclaimed by the Allies in the last war, plainly contravened this, and meant that that war was certainly not a just war. It is a blot on the good name of the Church that its leaders did not stand out against this at the time.

The traditional doctrine of the just war, with its strictly limited objectives, has led in practice to strong attempts—which have not been vain attempts—to restrict the ravages of war and, so far as possible, civilize it. Thus the Red

[1] S.T. 2a. 2ae. Q. 40. a. 1.

Cross and all that it implies is the direct outcome of these attempts. They are ultimately based upon the important distinction between *nocentes* and *innocentes* which has generally, though not accurately, been equated with the distinction between combatants and non-combatants. In fact, this has been a most unfortunate equation which has fatally blurred the accurate thinking of the old canonists. Consequently, there has grown up 'a hazy idea, quite unknown to the old law, that civilians form a kind of privileged order, and that any attack upon them, no matter what their activities may be, is inherently wrongful. The words of distinction used by the canonists and their successors are "guilty" and "innocent," and this language is based upon the conception of war as being in its essence a process for the enforcement of law. Those who oppose or obstruct the forces of justice are guilty persons and may be ruthlessly put out of the way. Those who take no part in resistance and continue to mind their ordinary business are individually innocent, and they should be exempt from direct attack, upon the principle that the innocent cannot be lawfully punished for the wrong done by others. . . . The following passage may be quoted from Vitoria: "Even in war with the Turks it is not permissible to kill children. This is clear because they are innocent; and the same applies to the women of unbelievers. In so far as war is concerned, women are presumed to be innocent, but this does not apply in the case of any individual woman who is certainly guilty. Among Christians the same holds good for harmless agricultural folk, and also for the rest of the peaceful population, since all these must be presumed innocent, until the contrary is shown." Grotius devotes a long chapter to the question of limitations (*temperamenta*) upon the right to kill in war. . . . Perhaps it is worth while to note what he says about women: they are entitled to immunity "unless they do something particularly reprehensible, such as taking men's jobs." [1] The canonists, however, are quite clear that when it is necessary for the attainment of victory to kill the innocent *incidentally*— e.g. in bombarding a fortress—this is lawful. It is at this point that we touch the nerve of the whole problem of war as it exists to-day. Since the introduction of atomic warfare, killing in war has become indiscriminate on such a vast scale as to threaten, and in the opinion of many Christians, to destroy, the whole conception of the just war.

The problem of atomic warfare as it exists at the present time seems to resolve itself into three main questions:

(*a*) Is the possession of atomic weapons, with readiness to use them without restriction if necessary, morally legitimate?

(*b*) Is the possession of atomic weapons simply and solely as a deterrent legitimate?

(*c*) Is it legitimate to use them not only as a deterrent but also, if used by the enemy, in self-defence?

We turn to the first of these three questions. This was, of course, what happened on the fateful 6 August, 1945, when Hiroshima was obliterated by the first atomic bomb. At the time there were a good many Christians who defended the action, although it is probably true to say that the majority were deeply shocked and condemned the action without qualification. Nevertheless, this action found its defenders. For example, the Commission of the British Council of Churches in its report, *The Era of Atomic Power*, refused to pronounce a unanimous condemnation. They wrote: 'Some of our members would have liked the Commission to associate itself with the American Commission in unqualified condemnation of the action. It seemed to others that they were not yet sufficiently aware of all the facts that had to be weighed by those in whose hands the

[1] Quoted from *The Church and the Atom*, pp. 62 and 63, the Report of a commission appointed by the Archbishops of Canterbury and York (1948).

decision rested to commit themselves to so clear-cut a
judgement.' Yet it is hard to see what further information
was required for the passing of judgement. The only
relevant fact was whether the enemy was in a position to
forestall them in this matter, if we had not acted quickly;
and it was known that this was not the case. The action was
definitely not directed by necessity. Moreover, Hiroshima
and Nagasaki were neither of them on the list of cities which
had been definitely warned against special air attacks. Yet
the condemnation was not made. The same applies to the
Lower House of the Convocation of Canterbury, when
after three separate attempts to make them face the issue,
the matter was finally shelved. It is, therefore, significant
that since that time Christian opinion has hardened against
the use of atomic weapons. It is true that most recent
atomic weapons are said to be many times more powerful
than the bombs dropped in 1945; but it is difficult to think
that this is the sole reason for the change in opinion. For it
is true that no sooner had the allies dropped these two
abominations than they began to cast about for ways to
ensure that nothing similar was likely to happen to themselves. At all events, it is almost certainly true to say that
this first question would be answered in the negative by the
vast majority of Christians to-day. They would in no un-
certain voice condemn absolutely the introduction of these
terrible weapons of indiscriminate slaughter into modern
warfare. So far as this issue is concerned, in the eyes of
Christians, there *is* no moral problem. The act is wicked
without qualification, and indistinguishable from mass
murder.

(*b*) We turn to our second question, Is the mere possession
of atomic weapons, solely as a deterrent, legitimate? Here
Christian opinion is divided. There are many who would
argue that since fear of reprisals is beyond question the most
effective deterrent in war—and it is, to say the least, arguable

that the possession of these weapons has already in fact prevented a major war from breaking out—it is not only legitimate, but the duty of the great powers to be in possession of these arms. As the authors of *The Era of Atomic Power* said: 'The weapon of the atomic bomb ought in the future be used for one purpose and one purpose alone, to deter by the threat, and if necessary by the execution, of reprisals a nation which attempted to use it for aggressive purposes.'[1] The words to which exception might be taken in this statement are 'and if necessary by the execution of.' It might be argued that if a nation decided to manufacture these weapons and keep them solely as a deterrent, nursing a secret intention never in any circumstances to use them, there could be no moral objection to them. Presumably there would be few Christians who would in this case condemn their manufacture, until there was mutual agreement among the nations to outlaw them. But of course it is true—to quote *The Era of Atomic Power* again—that 'it cannot be used as a deterrent without the *possibility* (italics mine) of an occasion arising when the threat of reprisal would have to be put into action.' It is this possibility which, for many Christians, completely undermines this second position, so that they would be compelled to answer this question, like the first, in the negative. On the other hand, 'unilateral disarmament,' in this matter, would make the rest of the world a prey and a victim of any power which possessed these arms.

(*c*) This brings us to the third question, and this is the most difficult as well as the most vitally important of the three questions in practice. Christian opinion is unfortunately at the present time sharply divided here. On the one side are those who answer this question, like the first two, with an unqualified No. As a representative of those who take this view, we may cite Professor Thomas Wood. He says:

[1] *Op. cit.*, p. 54.

'There may be circumstances in which the doctrine of "strict necessity" is applicable; but the use of hydrogen bombs reduces the doctrine of "strict necessity" to a phantom. For, in what sense could you be said to be acting in the defence of an ally if the inevitable consequence of your assistance with nuclear bombs must be to add to the wholesale devastation of its territory and the indiscriminate slaughter of its population? And in what sense could you be said to be defending the citizens of your country, their way of life, and their standard of values, if, by resorting to nuclear warfare against an aggressive and unscrupulous nuclear-armed power, your own country and the enemies' must be virtually reduced to ashes? The aim of a defensive war is to repel the enemy's unjust attack upon you (or your ally) and to restrain him from further evil. But to drop nuclear bombs at any stage of the conflict "would not be to restrain the enemy from further evil: it would be to destroy them utterly and in that destruction to destroy whatever is good in them and every hope of the triumph of that good." . . . Thus it would appear that even a war which began with a just cause and a right intention would cease to be a just war the moment a nuclear bomb was used: for, at that moment, recourse would be had to be a deliberate act of indiscriminate slaughter, and to be a measure of destruction, altogether disproportionate to the end which the war was being undertaken to achieve.'[1]

That is one answer to this tremendous moral question; yet I must confess that it does not satisfy me. When the first atomic bombs were dropped I was in no doubt in my own mind that those were right who condemned this as an act of brutality. I can, therefore, plead that I am not at all prejudiced in favour of atomic weapons. Nevertheless, I am not convinced by Professor Wood's argument: and that for two main reasons. The first is that it is not really possible

[1] T. Wood: *Some Moral Problems* (1961), p. 85.

to foresee the course or the consequences of an atomic war. Some argue that it would virtually destroy mankind. Others maintain that this is very far from being the case. We, therefore, have to be careful not to use exaggerated language in this matter. The second, and more weighty, reason is that, from the point of view of moral theology, we have to weigh in the scales two alternatives. What would be the alternative to the use of atomic weapons in self-defence? It would be total and *final* submission to an unprincipled aggressor. For, *ex hypothesi*, no nation would initiate an atomic war which did not fall under that category. This would entail the full and *final* surrender of all spiritual values and the establishment of a ruthless dictatorship by a power which could, and doubtless would, in time crush the Christian religion out of existence. We have to remember that such a thing is possible. It happened in Japan in the Middle Ages. Would the preservation of humanity for such a fate be to confer a benefit upon it and upon the children yet unborn? That seems to me to be the crucial question. In my view, the answer is No. If it should be that the other alternative is the virtual obliteration *physically* of the human race (and, as I have said, this is far from being certain) in my view that would be a lesser evil than the other alternative which would lead to the virtual obliteration of the human race *spiritually*. In other words, which is the lesser evil, that humanity should lose its body or its soul? It seems to me that, from the Christian point of view, there can be no doubt as to the answer to that dread question. It follows that in the last resort, it would be the lesser of two colossal evils for a nation to defend itself with nuclear weapons than to abjure their use, and thus fall into everlasting slavery.

In terms of moral theology, this position was very clearly expressed in *The Church and the Atom*. 'If one nation began hostilities against another by launching an attack with atomic weapons upon its principal cities, would a reply in kind be justified? To this we answer, first, that in all probability such an attack would by threatening the existence of the community subjected to it establish a "present imminent danger" which would justify all measures genuinely necessary to self-defence. Secondly, since in these circumstances the only hope of effective defence would lie in bringing overwhelming force to bear upon the enemy immediately, it seems that the use of atomic weapons would be genuinely necessary. Thirdly, since it would also be necessary to use these weapons in the most immediately efficacious way, whatever damage and casualties were inflicted in so doing would rightly be regarded as incidental to self-defence. If this answer is correct, we consider that any nation, or any group of nations, which was resolved to resist aggression of the kind supposed, should let it be known that it held itself entitled to defend itself in this way. In our judgement such warning might go far to prevent the abuse of atomic weapons.'[1]

---

[1] *The Church and the Atom:* A Study of the Moral and Theological Aspects of Peace and War. The Report of a Commission appointed by the Archbishops of Canterbury and York at the request of the Church Assembly to consider the Report of the British Council of Churches' Commission entitled 'The Era of Atomic Power' (1948), p. 52.

INDEX